Psychology Graduate School

A User's Manual

Steven R. Smith

University of California, Santa Barbara

ROWMAN & LITTLEFIELD

Lanham • Boulder • New York • London

Executive Editor: Nancy Roberts
Assistant Editor: Megan Manzano
Senior Marketing Manager: Amy Whitaker
Interior Designer: Ilze Lemesis

Credits and acknowledgments for material borrowed from other sources, and reproduced with permission, appear on the appropriate page within the text.

Published by Rowman & Littlefield
An imprint of The Rowman & Littlefield Publishing Group, Inc.
4501 Forbes Boulevard, Suite 200, Lanham, Maryland 20706
www.rowman.com

Unit A, Whitacre Mews, 26-34 Stannary Street, London SE11 4AB, United Kingdom

British Library Cataloguing in Publication Information Available

Library of Congress Cataloging-in-Publication Data

Names: Smith, Steven R., 1972– author.
Title: Psychology graduate school : a user's manual / Steven R. Smith,
    University of California, Santa Barbara.
Description: Lanham : Rowman & Littlefield, [2018] | Includes index.
Identifiers: LCCN 2018016714 (print) | LCCN 2018032252 (ebook) | ISBN
    9781538106600 (electronic) | ISBN 9781538106587 (cloth : alk. paper) |
    ISBN 9781538106594 (pbk. : alk. paper)
Subjects: LCSH: Psychology—Study and teaching (Graduate)—Handbooks,
    manuals, etc.
Classification: LCC BF77 (ebook) | LCC BF77 .S58 2018 (print) | DDC
    150.71/1—dc23
LC record available at https://lccn.loc.gov/2018016714

Dedication

For Stella

Contents

Preface

About a million years ago now, I admitted my first graduate student into the PhD program at UCSB. I was all of about five minutes older than she was, and we were both almost totally ignorant about what graduate school was supposed to be like (I only had my own graduate school experience to guide both of us). In the 14 years since then, I've learned a few things about what graduate school is *supposed* to be like and what it actually *is* like. In that time, I've learned about what parts of the journey tend to be difficult, which are exciting and fresh, and which are painful or unnerving. I can be a much better guide to my students now than I could have ever been back then. Thankfully, I have some capacity to learn things.

Although all grad students are brilliant (or at least clever enough to fool us into admitting them) and well prepared academically, most students have never done graduate school before and of course don't know what to expect. Over the years, I've often said that graduate school needs a user's manual. Your car has one, your microwave has one, and you can even find good manuals for how to keep your marriage together or raise a puppy that doesn't eat your shoes. Lots of books will teach you how to apply to grad school and generally do well with the academic, research, and clinical bits, but none of them really cut to the chase and tell you what grad school is like . . . *really* like. Instead of continuing to complain that there was no user's manual for graduate school, I decided to write one.

This book has at least three audiences: current graduate students in psychology, students who are planning to attend graduate school in psychology, and families or loved ones of graduate students in psychology who are trying to make sense of things from the outside. I pay particular attention to students in programs in counseling, school, and clinical psychology, in which there is a practice component. This does not exclude those who might be in IO, social, bio, or experimental psychology, because the experiences of these students are similar enough that there are still lessons to be had.

My hope is to share some of my personal experiences as a student and as a professor and to offer experiences of students who have gone before you. Throughout this book, you'll see several quotes from real graduate students from all over the country. In some cases, they've allowed me to use their first names, but other times they've chosen to remain anonymous. Heed their advice and consider their experiences—it's hard to get more real than that. You might also notice that some of their comments and suggestions are contradictory. It turns out that real people have differing experiences, so rather than trying to make everything neat to fit a general narrative, I've opted to capture a diversity of experience.

I'm thankful that Rowman & Littlefield has allowed me to write this in my own voice without having to be too formal. It was important to me to have a genuine voice as though I'm speaking to you the way I speak to graduate students. A book about the reality of graduate student life should be presented in a real voice. I hope it's not too distracting. In the few places where I discuss clinical information or stories about graduate students, I have changed a few details to mask identities.

This is the paragraph where I thank a bunch of people you don't know. First, I ran a number of chapter drafts past former graduate students Dr. Wendy Morrison, Dr. Robert Duff, Dr. Justin Gauthier, and Dr. Ilyssa Bass, with a particular shout-out to Dr. Ashley Sanford (who read lots and lots of chapters). These brilliant psychologists provided invaluable feedback on content, tone, and topics. Thanks to the faculty and administration of the PGSP-Stanford PsyD Consortium, where I started this project, and to UCSB, where I finished it. I'm indebted to Molly White and Nancy Roberts at Rowman & Littlefield for their support for the project and to the baristas at Good Cup Coffee in Santa Barbara for not kicking me out when I'd sit and write for hours after only buying one small tea.

Finally, and most important, I appreciate the wonderful, brilliant, and inspiring graduate students I've had over the years who have taught me how to be a professor. They are why I do what I do and why I love my job so much.

CHAPTER 1

Now I Actually Have to Go?!

Well, you did it! You got admitted to graduate school. Nicely done! You should be both proud and relieved. It's an indication that your hard work, diligence, and obsessively written cover letters have paid off. I remember opening my graduate school acceptance letter (delivered via mail on actual paper) and feeling an overwhelming sense of joy that was followed a short time later by an anxious realization that now I actually had to *go to graduate school*! And it turns out that my reaction wasn't so uncommon. If you're like me and a lot of other students before you, you've been so focused on getting *into* graduate school that you haven't really thought through what it would be like to actually *be* a graduate student.

> When I learned that I had been accepted to graduate school I felt an incredible sense of relief and excitement. It had been a lengthy and expensive process and I was happy to finally be able to stop worrying about whether or not I was going to be able make it into a PhD program. It was truly one of the most gratifying moments in my life.
>
> —Natalia, first-year public PhD student

> More important to me than my reaction was my mother's. When I called and told her the good news, she screamed, burst into tears, and said, "MY BABY'S GOING TO BE A DOCTOR!"
>
> —Sarah, second-year private PsyD student

What will it be like? Will the classes be hard? Will it be competitive? Are you ready for it? Do you really have to take *only* psychology classes? Will they find out that you don't really belong and that they made a mistake in admissions?

Luckily, I'm here to help. I survived graduate school and have lived on to become a real-life psychologist and professor of clinical psychology at a public,

American Psychological Association (APA)–accredited PhD program (I was also a professor at a private PsyD program for a few years). I have some things to share that might be useful in your transition from a nervous newbie with a gnarly case of imposter syndrome to a full-fledged psychologist with a gnarly case of imposter syndrome. The purpose of this book is to help guide you through the exciting and exacting process of graduate school, including how your faculty make sense of the world, what to expect from starting research and clinical work, and how to navigate the internship process without going nuts. This book will be of interest to folks who have already been admitted to grad school and even those contemplating attendance. Research tells us that knowing what's ahead helps to reduce anxiety and increase preparedness. It's in that spirit that this book is offered.

How Graduate School Is Different From Undergraduate School

When you think about how grad school will be different from your undergraduate studies, what comes to mind? Harder classes? Cooler frat parties? More work? More independent work? More writing? Of course, your answer depends on what type of undergraduate institution you attended, but many students are surprised at some of the differences between grad and undergrad in psychology. Here are the primary highlights that most students seem to notice:

1. All you do is psychology. If you're like me, as an undergrad you took psychology courses, but you also took a lot of nonpsychology courses. I took English courses, sociology, dance, philosophy, and political science courses. I had a minor in criminal justice and nearly enough courses to have a second minor in English. Before I started, I never thought about the fact that, as a grad student, all I would take is psychology. Sure, statistics courses broke up the days a bit so it didn't feel like I was only reading about the vagaries of human behavior, but the "liberal artsy" part of my mind that craved interdisciplinary dialogue and stretching boundaries wasn't satisfied in the same way during grad school. (Because I had a tuition waiver, I looked into taking a scuba course in grad school, but I couldn't afford the equipment fee, so I slunk back to the psychology building in defeat.) All psychology, all the time.

2. Because all you do is psychology, it feels more like a job than school. Your days are long, there are lots of things to accomplish, and a lot of those things are tedious. Very little of your time is scheduled with *things*, but all of your time is filled. If you think of it as a job, it gives you a performance mentality, which is helpful in navigating relationships with faculty and peers (more on that in the chapters to follow). The other reason to think of it like a job is because it will help you set limits. No one wants to set limits on their *education*, but a *job*? Yeah, boundaries are good.

3. Grades don't matter. Really. Seriously. I kid you not. I mean, if you get a C, most grad programs consider that a failure, but apart from that, grades

don't matter. Internship programs might look at your transcripts to make sure that you've taken a particular course, but survey data suggest that internship directors consider grades one of the least important parts of a student's application. And after internship, it's doubtful that anyone will ever want to see a copy of your transcript again for as long as you live. I've taught graduate seminars where there were *no graded assignments*! Your grad professors expect you to do the work, and they expect you to do it well. That makes grades somewhat unnecessary and redundant. Hopefully they'll give you good feedback on your work, but chances are that if you do what's required, you'll be fine. What this all means is that if you're debating an all-nighter to turn a B into an A (possibly at the expense of being alert and ready for practicum or statistics class), take the B with a smile. As we said in my grad program, "Bs get degrees."

Try not to get lost in the details of the process. Trust that it will begin to unfold in front of you if you genuinely engage.

—Natalie, third-year private PsyD student

---

4. **The work isn't harder, but there's often more of it (with little to show for it).** As a new grad student, I was surprised that I wasn't challenged by the difficulty of the material. Stats wasn't harder stats than I had as an undergrad, papers weren't harder papers, and the readings weren't harder readings, but there were a lot more of them. At some point, you'll look at all the reading you have been assigned for a given week and you'll realize that it's not possible to complete it and still sleep, eat, and maintain basic personal hygiene. You'll need to begin to make choices about what work you'll actually do and what work you'll skip or just half-ass (and don't forgo personal hygiene). Part of the challenge of grad school is that you'll need to learn how to learn efficiently and in broad strokes. Part of that process is deciding what to totally skip or when a crappy job is good enough. It's like a giant salad bar: if you eat all of everything, you'll get sick, but if you sample a little bit of everything, you'll have less gastric distress. And to borrow an image from the Beatles, grad school is like trying to catch a rainstorm in a paper cup: you can only get what you can get. If you miss something important, you can come back to it later.

The hardest adjustment for me was school and life balance. There's an endless amount of readings and opportunities in graduate school, and it's easy to let self-care fall to the wayside.

—Sarah, second-year private PsyD student

Learn to advocate for yourself early and often. If there's something you want, be confident in your ability to make it happen for yourself. If there is something you don't want, be confident in your ability to say "no." I say this, of course, still working on it myself.

—Meg, second-year public PhD student

Advocate for yourself. If you want your advisor's time and attention, ask for it. If you're not sure what's going on in class or what's expected of you in regard to an assignment, raise your hand or talk to the professor or TA after class. Never hesitate to ask for the things that are going to help you succeed.

—First-year public PhD student

5. In grad school, relationships matter a lot more. At times, your grad school program can feel a lot like a fishbowl. Most programs (particularly PhD programs) are pretty small, with only 10 or fewer students admitted each year to work with 10–15 faculty. Given that nearly all doctoral programs require four years of on-campus study, that means you'll be spending a lot of time with the same people in a lot of different contexts: classrooms, office space, research labs, practica, and even carpooling and apartment sharing. If you went to a larger undergraduate institution, you could be relatively anonymous. Not so with grad school. If you have a bad day or a bad breakup, or are struggling in some way, people will know, and they'll talk about it. You'll need to navigate the moods of the faculty (and some of us are very moody) and have some understanding of the parts of their jobs that are stressful. You'll likely make some of the very best friends you'll have in your life, but you'll also need to navigate the complexities of all those relationships. And although these are useful life skills to have, it can get tiring (particularly if you're used to doing your own thing).

It is very difficult to become close to people, including my cohort. Everyone is busy with their own work and don't make socializing a priority, even though, in my opinion, it is important to form close relationships when you are going through something so difficult.

—First-year public PhD student

When you feel like you're the only one who is overwhelmed, I guarantee everyone else in your cohort is feeling the same way but no one wants to admit it. Form relationships with those in your cohort because those are the faces you're going to be seeing all the time.

—Jacqueline, second-year public MA student

6. As opposed to undergrad school, you'll need to be more self-directed. Stated differently, more of the work of graduate school is independent. The journey of graduate school is toward *independent practice*, which means that you'll need to practice independence. Classes and practica can only teach you so much about clinical practice and theory, so you'll buy books or check them out from the library (it's the big building on campus with all the books in it; people used to go there a lot before the internet). You'll find a research topic that's of interest, so you'll do lit searches for journal articles to read. No one will (likely) tell you to do this, but that's where a lot of the learning comes from. Also, once you hit the dissertation or thesis stage, you'll be working on projects completely different from those of your classmates, and you'll need to be bullish with your own timelines, processes, and work ethic. If you wait for someone to tell you what to do, you'll be in grad school forever, and if you wait for someone to teach you what you need to know, you won't learn what you should. If you like to work independently, you can rejoice. But if you're challenged by a lack of externally imposed deadlines, you'll need to develop some self-regulatory skills pretty quickly.

Grad school for me is a self-taught enterprise. If I'm interested in something, I have to be a go-getter and get it done myself. Advisors are so busy. Peers in lab are busy. You're busy. It can feel disheartening that no one is really mentoring you, but you have to go out and find those mentors, find those resources and hold on to them with both hands.

—First-year public PhD student

---

7. If you're in a program that involves clinical work, you'll be surprised at how much you have to *think about yourself*. Graduate school and especially the start of clinical work forces you to think deeply about yourself in a way that you probably never have before. You'll reconsider stories from your childhood, weird behaviors you have, your goofball family, and your closest interpersonal relationships. As clinical supervisors probe into your reactions to your patients, you'll be forced to grapple with your unconscious experiences and reactions as well as your implicit biases regarding diversity factors and the like. Also, given that many (if not most) graduate students seek out personal therapy, you might find yourself spending a lot of time in therapy, as a therapist, and as a student dealing with your internal landscape in ways you haven't before. I remember saying to a friend in grad school, "Sure, those chemistry doc students spend a lot of time in the lab, but they don't need to deal with all this 'painful self-reflection' nonsense."

It sounds really corny, but honestly I feel that the thing I am most proud of in grad school is just growing up. The pressures of the program kind of forced me to introspect—at times, painfully—about how I spend my time and the choices that I am making in building a professional future for myself. And in order to act with my values (and avoid being completely hypocritical with my clients), I ended up letting go of a lot of the insecurities and self-sabotaging tendencies that had defined earlier phases of my life . . . basically because there was no room for that anymore. You can't really get the job done without putting your whole heart into it.

—Evelyn, fourth-year public PhD student

I realized that I don't need to change just because I'm in the upper echelon of education. My personality, my sense of humor, my morals are all an inherent part of who I am and I need to keep rediscovering pride in those things.

—First-year public PhD student

· · · · · · · · · · · · · · · · · · **Words of Wisdom** · · · · · · · · · · · · · · · · · ·

1. The admissions committee did not make a mistake. If you're in graduate school, you deserve to be there.
2. The imposter syndrome is normal. Get used to it because it never goes away (it just changes form).
3. Everyone is stressed and trying to make a good impression.
4. The hardest work in graduate school is the internal work. Get ready for some "painful self-reflection nonsense."

· ·

Settling In and Getting Started

The first quarter or semester of graduate school can be one of the most challenging. Often you'll have to move to a new town, separating from friends, family, and familiarity. Along with setting up a new place to live, new routines, and perhaps even a new state residency, you need to settle into graduate school and the role of being a graduate student. This challenge is even greater for international students who might still be learning idioms of language, cultural differences, and so forth. And if you're a graduate student who is coming back to school after time in the "real world," readjusting to the role of a student can be a real shocker. By doing a little legwork first, you can ease that transition in a way that might be helpful in the future.

The transition to graduate school was surprisingly easier than I had anticipated. I had all these terrifying ideas about how awful it was going to be. But once I compartmentalized my tasks and assignments, tried my best, and met necessary deadlines, everything felt manageable.

—Reycine, second-year private PsyD student

The friendships and support network I gained from people in my program were helpful in adjusting to graduate school. Since we are all going through the same thing, they really understand the challenges and can provide empathy or advice. My undergraduate preparation in critical thinking/writing and the research skills I gained from a year of working after graduation have been really helpful as well.

—Meg, second-year public PhD student

I felt lonely when I first started graduate school. I felt distanced from my friends who were working and disheartened by any competitiveness that I sensed from my peers. I found the demands on my time to be overwhelming. I felt that I was constantly being told to relax and be easygoing while being told to do more or else I would fall behind. The stress deepened feelings of loneliness and isolation.

—Second-year private PsyD student

I was really alone. I didn't know anyone. My family is hours away. It was lonely, and entering into grad school for the first weeks, most of the people in my cohort, myself included, were still trying to present this face that everything was fine and everything was perfect: Wasn't the weather so great? Wasn't the program so perfect? Wasn't life so grand? Isn't grad school such a breeze? But I didn't feel like that AT ALL. I was really sad at first. I missed my friends. I hadn't been without a social support group for a long time, and knowing that I couldn't be myself right away was hard.

—First-year public PhD student

First, remember that you're a part of at least two communities: the university community and the local community. At the beginning of the academic year, the university community will likely welcome you with an exhaustive list of orientation activities. Department orientation, grad student orientation, teaching assistant orientation, international student orientation, graduate student women orientation, research funding orientation, HIPAA training, technology training, and other nearly endless varieties of "getting to know you" social events will populate the first few weeks of your time. Go to the ones you need and want to, but ask advanced students whether there are some places where you can save some energy and get caught up on Netflix.

My feeling is that too few graduate students get involved in the larger university community (if there is one). Undergrads seem to easily find their way to various clubs and organizations, but grad students often seem hesitant to jump in. Perhaps that's because of a "busyness" factor, age differences, or a sense that they've been there and done that, but I think campus involvement can be really energizing. Graduate students, because of both age and experience, have a lot to offer university discourse on political, social, and cultural issues. Even sports and social clubs can use your help. You can be a helpful voice of maturity. Likewise, it helps grad students feel a sense of the larger community and not so cooped up in the psychology building, the lab, or the library (the building with the books). And, socially, I think it's very important to have friends outside of the departmental fishbowl to help keep you from going nuts. As a student, I was once walking across campus and someone asked me for directions to such-and-such building. "I have no idea," I replied, "I'm a grad student."

> I did not expect to feel so isolated from the rest of the university community (undergrad, other programs, etc.). I did not feel that way in undergrad. It's certainly different.
>
> —Reycine, second-year private PsyD student

Although I didn't know my way around campus, I did know my way around town, because I was very much a member of the local community. Regardless of how you fit in with the campus community, consider getting involved with the local community. If you identify with a religion, seek out a congregation. If you participate in a sport, seek out local sports clubs. If you are politically minded, seek out local activist groups. Finally, if there's a local psychological association, join it as a student affiliate (usually only a couple of bucks). Remember, graduate school feels like a job, so if you can connect with other people who are working jobs, you'll likely have more in common than you will with undergraduates. Connecting with the community can have a real normalizing effect on the nonnormal activities of graduate school.

Most of my friends in grad school were not other graduate students but people I met in town through my sport activities. I spent my time with folks who worked in retail, tech, health care, and banking. They had spouses, children, pets, mortgages, and other grown-up stuff. And their real-world issues and concerns were a nice antidote to the goofiness of grad student life and reminded me how good I had it. I could complain to them about the vagaries of professors, comprehensive exams, university red tape, and student colleagues, and they were a good source of support and a reminder that not everything is as weird as grad school. Invest in your community; you'll be there for at least four years, so there's time to grow at least some small roots and forge some really good relationships.

> Even though graduate school work is important, I didn't give up also having a life outside of school. Being able to find a balance between work and play helped to put my mind on pause and not to forget what else I still loved to enjoy in life. I took up new hobbies and got involved in other ways outside my program to still keep me busy but include an added element of fun among all the stress.
>
> —Jacqueline, second-year public MA student

In the spirit of making friends and settling into the university community, make friends with your reference librarian. Pardon me for sounding like a cranky old professor here, but "kids these days ain't got no library skills." Most of you have grown up with ready access to the internet, but, as a graduate student, you need to be more discerning about where your information comes from. As I often say to students, "Google isn't a literature search." I suggest you go to your library and get a course in scientific literature searches (most libraries offer courses like this). Honestly, it will save you time later on because you won't need to wade through the misinformation that poses as information, and your professors will be pleased that you've cited *good* sources. In a thesis or dissertation, you'll need to conduct an *exhaustive* literature search, so knowing how to go about that in a structured and organized way will be a handy skill to have. Most academic librarians have either master's degrees or even doctorates in library science, so it's clear that they have something to teach you.

In terms of settling into the academic portion of your journey, learn how to work "smart, not hard." Actually, you'll work plenty hard, so it's even more important that you work smart. Like I mentioned above, there's no way you can do all the work you're assigned. Work with your student colleagues to spread the work around in whatever way you choose, read some things deeply and others in a more cursory manner (or not at all), don't do extra credit unless you need to, and spend more time with things that you're really interested in, even if that means you'll lose a few points elsewhere. It's important that you approach graduate school as a somewhat selfish enterprise where your focus should be on your *education* rather than on externally imposed markers of success.

To be clear, you can't completely ignore grades and evaluation, but I encourage you to be passionate about *learning* more than you're passionate about *achieving*. The irony here, of course, is that *achievement* is what got you into grad school: grades, GREs, and all the extracurricular research and clinical experiences are often driven by an achievement orientation. And you've also had to be competitive to get picked from the hundreds of other applicants. But at this point in the game, you need to resist those very things. Most graduate programs will frown upon students who are too competitive (it makes for crappy relationships with peers, too) or too achievement oriented. The reason that I know this is that *I* was one of those students: too competitive and too achievement oriented. Looking back now as a professor, I'm clear that I was likely an insufferable and obnoxious student. And in retrospect, I regret that I was unable to learn as much as I could from peers and faculty. Don't be like me; be a humble learner.

I'm a single mom of a seven-year-old boy and work as a paralegal for a family law attorney, so the hardest part for me has been learning how to juggle it all. The first quarter I had too many balls in the air and quickly realized that I wasn't going to be able to keep that act up for long without losing my mind. I scaled back at work this quarter and have gotten better at figuring out how to prioritize school, and so far it is going MUCH better than my first quarter.

—Emily, first-year public MA student

A quick word here about pets: Over the years, I've witnessed what I call *first-year dog syndrome*. Given the stress of the grad school transition and the loneliness that often comes with it, I've seen a disproportionate number of students rush out to adopt dogs (and cats) in their first year of grad school (this is less of a phenomenon in urban graduate programs). I speak from experience; I did it too. I suggest that you resist this urge, at least for the first year. What's hard to anticipate is that, during your first year, you spend a lot of time in your dorm, apartment, basement, or flophouse studying and reading. There's lots of alone time in your space. In that context, it makes sense to get a pet. However, in the later years of school, you won't be home that much because you'll be doing clinical work or research on campus or in the community. Your dog will be upset, and you'll have to make weird compromises to make sure his needs are met. Then, in your fifth or sixth year, you'll need to pack up and move to another place that might not be so dog friendly (I could tell you horror stories of looking for dog-friendly apartments in Boston!), and then, after all that, you'll probably need to move again for postdoc, and then you'll move again for your first job. If you're committed to getting a dog, then go for it—just realize that you're assigning both him and you to a nomadic few years where you'll be busy and often out of the house. Cats are less needy, and cat-friendly apartments are easier to find, so I think they're a better bet; fish are even better.

That said, the comfort of a pet can be really reassuring and help with feelings of loneliness and stress. And nothing (other than a child) can teach you more about compromise and caring, skills that will serve you well in many contexts. My point is to choose carefully and consider where you'd like to live in seven or eight years.

My dog was super helpful in my transition to grad school, cheesy though that may sound. Having a pet and therefore having something that loves you unconditionally and cares if you're stressed out and doesn't judge you if you're not at your best was totally helpful in making me realize that I don't have to be a perfect automaton. It's OK to be a person, have faults, and struggle. Really my dog helped me realize that my experience was normal in that it was mine and nothing else really mattered.

—First-year public PhD student

Imposter Syndrome

Each year at new student orientation, I have the pleasure of standing in a room of brand-new graduate students, all of whom are brilliant hard workers who have distinguished themselves personally, professionally, and academically. Each one is as impressive as the next, and the diversity of impressiveness is a joy to witness. Having sat on graduate admissions for the past 13 years, I can attest to the fact that those students were chosen carefully and thoughtfully. They all deserve to be there. If you're a graduate student, you deserve to be there too.

My hunch is that many of the students in that room are having a different experience than I am. As a new student, you enter a room full of talented people who have accomplished amazing things and excelled academically as much as you have (and sometimes more!). As you sit and listen to their stories about what they've done and where they're from, you might begin to have a creeping (if not terrifying) sense of anxiety: Did the admissions committee make a mistake? Do I belong here? What happens when they find out that I'm not as smart as these other folks? If I vomited on my orientation materials, would anyone notice? That, my friend, is the voice of *imposter syndrome* (IS). Make friends with that voice because you'll have it for a long, long time. I often say that imposter syndrome never goes away; you just get paid more for having it. Even in writing this book, I wonder whether I have the authority and experience to give you helpful information. There are many professors who have been around longer than I have, so who am I to pretend to be the authority on what grad school is like? Maybe I should just bag this whole thing right now and go watch Netflix because I'm clearly not qualified. . . .

In my first year as a graduate student, I find that it is very easy to get caught up comparing myself to the other people in my cohort. If I hear someone is going to a specific conference or is doing work for an organization, I immediately wonder if I should also be doing the same thing that they are and worry that I might be falling behind because I have been working on other aspects of my career. I constantly have to remind myself that everyone in the cohort has their own professional trajectory and I have to focus on my own projects and personal goals.

—Natalia, first-year public PhD student

Most people forget that as a first-year student, you don't really know anything. It was difficult to stay up to speed with what was going on in classes, my lab, and any other obligations.

—First-year public PhD student

OK, so, keeping my own imposter syndrome in check, let's look at some ways that IS can trip you up. In my mind, the greatest danger of imposter syndrome is overcorrection. Acting from a place of insecurity rarely brings about good results, so if you keep trying to prove that you belong (when your faculty already know you do), then you run the risk of driving everyone crazy. In class, don't always be the first to respond to a question, and don't waste time by trying to appear too clever or smart. Those sorts of things will be pretty apparent to the faculty and will irritate them more than impress them. Remember, graduate school is about relationships. Chill.

Be honest with your advisor. If you feel the pressure to pretend like you're han-
dling everything with ease so you don't look bad, STOP. The more honest you are
to your advisor, the better they can help you get the most out of your experience! You're not supposed to do this on your own.

—Sarah, second-year private PsyD student

The other hobgoblin of IS is that it might keep you from asking for help
when you need it. I've heard graduate students talk about not wanting to ask
too many questions because they don't want to appear ignorant to faculty or
advanced students. Ask questions when you don't know, even if you feel you
should. To be clear, make sure that you've done your homework and (at least
some of) the readings for class so you don't ask about something you should
know from homework. However, if you don't understand something, or if your
research advisor asks you offhand to do a power analysis for a given study (and
you think that power analysis might have something to do with how much you
can bench-press), then ask, and ask proudly.

Like I said, IS will crop up frequently, particularly when starting something
new. The imposter syndrome voice of anxiety can, of course, be really helpful
when you start clinical work or give your first few conference presentations. In
those situations, you need to be sure to bring your A game, so the sense that you
have no idea what you're doing can help you prepare, help you perform, and
give you a needed hunger to improve. Do you remember the Yerkes-Dodson
curve (Yerkes & Dodson, 1908)? Too little arousal or too much arousal will
work against you, so a little (but not too much) of that imposter syndrome
mojo can go a long way.

In my first year of graduate school, I learned that I am capable of balancing
much more than I thought. Grad school can push you to the limits of insanity
with the sheer number of things you have on your plate. But now I'm a scheduling boss! And still completely sane (though somewhat debatable).

—Reycine, second-year private PsyD student

In my first year of graduate school I learned that, even within a small group of
overachieving psychology nerds, there is so much diversity and an impossibly
vast range of experiences that we all benefit from learning about, and that my
experiences contribute to that, and are valuable.

—Sarah, second-year private PsyD student

In the first year of graduate school I learned that I had a softer heart than
I thought. I did not learn to be right more often. I learned to accept not being

right. I expanded the gray area between right and wrong, between I can and I cannot. I felt more comfortable with uncertainty and confident in discomfort.

—Natalie, third-year private PsyD student

I have learned that I am most productive in my work when I am able to make a little time for my hobbies, activities, and friendships. I have learned that if I want to be successful in my academics, I also need to find a way to prioritize my personal life because it helps me to stay grounded and positive.

—Natalia, first-year public PhD student

· · · · · · · · · · · · · · · · · **Tips and Strategies** · · · · · · · · · · · · · · · · ·

1. Make friends with people outside of your department so not all of your conversations are about nerdy psychology stuff.
2. Settle into your communities: the university and the local scene.
3. Arrange to spend some time with your reference librarian.
4. Focus on learning, not achieving.
5. Don't wait on someone to teach you. Seek out what you need and want to know.

· ·

If you've been accepted to graduate school, let me congratulate you again. No matter what, it'll be a wild ride full of challenging, fun, and fulfilling experiences. Settling into the graduate school waters can be a struggle, but it's good and important to start off on the right foot, with the right resources, and with a helpful mind-set. Enjoy this first step of your journey and try to remember the excitement that you feel at the beginning (because those memories will buoy you when stuff gets real).

Reference

Yerkes, R. M., & Dodson, J. D. (1908). The relation of strength of stimulus to rapidity of habit-formation. *Journal of Comparative Neurology and Psychology, 18,* 459–482.

CHAPTER 2

Those Who Can, Do
Making Sense of Your Professors

I love my job. But a few years into my academic career, I realized that, like a long-term prisoner, I could no longer make it "on the outside." When I talked to my business-world friends about faculty meetings where we discussed *processes* and *consensus*, they stared at me in disbelief. The real world works faster, more efficiently, and more decisively than academia ever will. And that's the way it should be. Academia is the holder of careful analysis, data-based decision making, and a progressive vision for our world. I'll argue forever that academia has an important role in our society, but it's a role that comes with a price tag of time and (often) efficiency.

As a graduate student, you're a part of that system, and those who are helping you along on the journey are part of that system. You may get frustrated by how long things take, but that's part of "academic speed" and doesn't necessarily mean that you've been forgotten or lost in the system. Your professors will have a higher capacity to tolerate this arrangement than you, so some may not be quick to recall that you might feel lost at times. I'll get back to this point later, but, first, let's try to sort through some terms.

Institution Types

Part of understanding faculty is knowing the type of institution they're in as well as the types of degrees offered there. There are many combinations of private versus public and research-oriented versus practice-oriented institutions. Most public universities and larger private universities tend to have a research focus where faculty success is often tied to grant writing and research productivity. Many smaller private universities and professional schools (i.e., universities that only offer a few professional degrees, perhaps in psychology, law, and/or business) tend to be somewhat more focused on the education and training of students over research productivity. The type of university tends to dictate the relative stresses and requirements of the job. In a research-focused university (public or private), faculty research record is the sine qua non of advancement and promotion, but in smaller private universities and professional schools, teaching and mentoring might be a greater priority for faculty time.

Faculty Types

No matter what type of university you're in, you might be tempted to think that all professors in your program have the same job, but that's likely not true. Your professors' jobs are largely dictated by the type of appointment they have as well as their rank. Given that you'll be living in the fishbowl with these people, it might behoove you to figure out what *kind* of faculty you have and, particularly if you're in a mentorship-model program, what *rank* your major professor might be. The reason this might be important is that it might help you know what to expect of them and, more important, what they might expect of you. Now, all of the terms I'm about to describe are a little hazy. Each university determines what kind of faculty it has and what the requirements are for advancement. Although I can offer a few descriptions of what's most typical, this is by no means an exhaustive list of all the varieties of faculty and their ranks.

First, there are lots of different *types* of faculty. If you're in a typical PhD program in a university, the chances are that most (but not all) of your faculty are *tenure-track professors*. In most places, tenure-track professors have doctorate degrees and are evaluated on research, teaching, and service (in that order). Promotion and advancement for these professors is largely based on their research productivity, and their teaching can be relatively (or substantially) secondary. Tenure-track faculty face pressures to publish research, write grants, present at conferences, and establish a recognizable trajectory of work. A professor with a large research grant might get bought out of teaching such that the grant pays the home department enough to hire an adjunct to teach his or her courses.

It should be noted that many universities are doing away with tenure (or at least offering tenure-track positions on a limited basis). Non-tenure-track faculty are on yearly contracts and, depending on the type of work they're contracted to do, might have a primary focus on research or teaching. If your faculty is largely composed of non-tenure-track faculty, they might always be nervous about getting let go without much notice. It's a rough gig, but, to be fair, it's more like a real job where you can actually be let go for subpar performance or financial exigencies.

In many institutions, there are also faculty who have a primarily responsibility for teaching rather than research. These appointment tracks are often known by titles like *teacher-scholar, teaching professor, educator*, or *lecturer*. If you're in a PsyD program or many terminal master's degree programs, it's likely that many of your faculty are teaching faculty rather than tenure-track research faculty. Many of these appointments have secure appointments akin to tenure (meaning that it's hard to fire them after they've proven themselves, as is true for a tenured professor). Often, these faculty have the same titles as their tenure-track counterparts (e.g., assistant professor, associate professor, etc.), so it might be tricky to tell the difference. For example, a certain professor might be an associate professor on the teacher-scholar line. The primary difference, of course, between a tenure-track research faculty and a lecturer or teacher-scholar is the ratio of teaching to research. Teaching faculty tend to teach more and have fewer expectations to publish (and there are often different standards for what counts as "scholarship").

If your school or program is affiliated with a medical school, you might have *clinical faculty*. Clinical faculty often have appointments to the medical school, but not to the wider university. They usually have some teaching and supervision responsibilities, but their primary job is clinical practice in a teaching clinic or hospital. Ironically (or at least it seems so to me), in order to get promoted as a clinical faculty member, they often have to demonstrate research productivity (even when they may have little time to do so). For example, when I was a staff psychologist at Massachusetts General Hospital (a Harvard Medical School teaching hospital), I also had a clinical faculty appointment to Harvard Med (which sounds more impressive than it was). Even if you're not in a medical school, you might have clinical faculty who run your department's training clinic or provide practicum supervision.

Many departments couldn't operate without *instructors* or *adjunct professors*. Adjuncts are often the unsung heroes of academia, and if you have any adjuncts as teachers or supervisors, be sure to thank them profusely and send them a birthday card. Usually adjuncts are at either the very beginning or the mid- to late parts of their careers. Beginning psychologists often do adjunct teaching to get some experience and make a few bucks while applying for academic or clinical jobs or starting a private practice. Later-career psychologists often pick up adjunct roles because they love being around bright and interesting graduate students. In either case, they're getting paid squat, they're often an afterthought for the university, and their future as teachers is uncertain from one semester to the next. However, you might find some of the best and most passionate teachers among the adjunct ranks. If you have a good adjunct, let them (and the department as a whole) know about it so they'll be asked back.

There are other, endless types of faculty appointments that a university can offer depending on the type of institution it is and what its needs are. Your department might also have *research faculty* (who usually don't teach at all), *clinical educators* (who only supervise clinical work), *visiting faculty* (who, obviously, are visiting from somewhere else), or *endowed chairs* (faculty who are appointed to a special faculty line that is usually funded by a rich donor or some such). The most senior professors in your department usually have *emeritus* status, meaning that they're more or less retired from active duty (in my mind, if emeritus faculty are doing it right, you'll never see them because they'll be out enjoying their retirement!). Spending a little time on figuring out who your professors are might be both useful and interesting for you (particularly if you're headed toward a career in academia).

Faculty Ranks

Now that we've covered the primary types of faculty, let's talk about ranks.[1] Tenure-track faculty (and teaching faculty in most institutions) have ranks that might be familiar to you: assistant professor, associate professor, and full professor. Fresh, new professors are hired at the assistant level. The assistant level

---

[1] As opposed to *rank*, which is often how nontenured faculty smell after a few too many late nights with data spreadsheets.

is considered a *probationary period*, such that these faculty are working toward tenure. Typically, the assistant period lasts for six or so years, at which time they can (or must) be evaluated for promotion.

Associate professors have crossed the tenure barrier and have secure appointments (unless they do something really bad or are total deadbeats). The jump from assistant or associate professor is often a challenging time for faculty. It certainly was a bumpy time for me. The promotion process is incredibly involved. Faculty are evaluated based on the number and quality of their publications, the number of grants they've written and/or received, the coherence of their research trajectories, their teaching evaluations, and their participation in university and national service. In addition to reviewing the professor directly, the university solicits reviews from a number of professors at other universities to evaluate their work. Those external reviewers submit letters of evaluation that are included with the candidate's self-statement, vitae, and supporting documents. Finally, the faculty is evaluated by several levels of the university, including the department, the dean, a standing personnel committee, and finally the university president or provost. It's likely that the whole evaluation process takes about a year or more. And in most institutions, if a professor does not get promoted to associate, their contracts terminate a short time later (usually a year). Some universities allow for an appeal or a reapplication to tenure after a year or two, but many don't. So, you can see why the assistant professors in your program might be stressed!

Associate professors are tenured faculty who have demonstrated competence in research and, to a lesser extent, teaching. Professors at this level are still very productive in research and might be taking time to establish a new interest or line of work. Often associate professors will go on sabbatical to help refresh and recharge their batteries and jump-start the next phase of their careers. Most universities will expect associate professors to be increasingly active in service activities, including serving as department chairs or chairs of committees in addition to working toward leadership positions in national or international professional organizations.

So, how do associate professors make the jump to full professor? It's the same type of process all over again: external letters, evaluation statements, research productivity, and deans. By the time a faculty member reaches the point of being a full professor in the tenure-track line, they're expected to be a leader (or emerging leader) in their field of research. Teaching faculty are expected to demonstrate teaching effectiveness across their course loads as well as a record of producing research and scholarship. Full faculty usually have more senior positions of leadership in the university or in the department and might be heavily involved in administration and leadership.

Faculty Service

Faculty have responsibilities in research, teaching, and service. Research and teaching are easy for most students to understand and see, but service is the secret time hobgoblin that students often don't have a sense of. No matter the size, academic programs have a nearly endless list of committees that keep things running: committees related to clinical training, curriculum, personnel, student affairs, funding, and general departmental operations. Academic departments are often housed in larger academic units called *schools* or *colleges* (e.g., a College of Letters and Sciences). Schools and colleges will also have their fair share of committees, like the committee on undergraduate education, diversity committees, or committees related to grants and funding. Finally, the university will have another slate of committees related to education, research, personnel, judicial affairs, diversity, admissions, and so forth. Here at UCSB, we even have a Committee on Committees (yes, really). Your professors are on many of these committees, which often meet a lot and have a lot of related work that's nearly invisible to the student body, but they keep the university running.

I believe that a faculty member's job consists of teaching, mentoring, applying for grants, conducting research, and attending meetings.

—Natalia, first-year public PhD student

In addition to university-based service, faculty are expected to engage in service to the profession. Professional service includes journal reviewing, leadership positions in national organizations, reviewing conference or grant submissions, or consulting with service or other organizations. Most places do not count clinical practice (e.g., professors with a private psychotherapy practice) as professional service. If it all sounds exhausting, it is.

It's really important to understand the service component of faculty work life because that's where a lot of time and energy disappears. The upside for students is that those professional relationships your faculty have can often come in handy when applying for jobs or internships. Faculty service also helps them keep abreast of university or field-related changes that might affect your education or education funding. When I look at my vitae, I count that I've been on 19 departmental or university committees (one of which I've been on for 12 years!), I've held 5 leadership positions in national organizations, and I've reviewed articles for at least 16 journals (I lost count of those somewhere). Many of these service activities were really fun and informative, and many were a drag, but, in either case, it's a huge part of my job and that of your professors too.

Teaching

When my wife and I were first dating, she asked me what I taught. "Students!" I replied. It's a wonder she wasn't through with me with right then. Indeed, I teach students, and it's the very best part of my job (except for the grading . . . that part blows). Teaching is exciting. It keeps us up to date on the latest developments in the field, and it allows us to spend time with brilliant graduate and undergraduate students.

And teaching is difficult. Despite being a huge part of our jobs, very few of us have any formal education in teaching. In grad school, I wasn't offered a course on pedagogy. They just handed me a textbook, a box of chalk, and told me when my classes met. My guess is that this experience is pretty typical. Of course, we've all had a lot of professors, and perhaps the best instruction is modeling. But still, it's a tough job, and flying blind never helps.

I was surprised how much work it was to design a class from scratch.

—Full professor, private PsyD program

A faculty member's job is to teach their subject matter in such a way that students are enthralled and excited to learn. They should connect their material to real-life applications and incorporate multicultural perspectives as much as possible. They should also care about and support the academic and professional growth of their students.

—Reycine, second-year private PsyD student

The challenge with faculty is that they often ignore the fact that as graduate students we have so much work and responsibilities. They want us to be fully immersed in their class while practicing self-care, but they neglect the fact that we are drowning with other responsibilities.

—First-year public PhD student

Consider the task of teaching. If your professor is teaching a course in her area of expertise, she must wrangle all of the knowledge that she has, distill it down into teachable units, and then assemble those units into a quarter or semester-long class. If that's the case, she's also *not* teaching you about as much stuff as she's teaching you. When I first started teaching personality assessment, I remember thinking, *How can the students understand any of this modern literature if they don't read this obscure series of articles from the 1940s? And item response theory? And theories of cultural identity formation?* And the list goes on. What all of this means for you is that the first few offerings of a course can be a little bumpy as a professor figures out what works and what doesn't. And it can also mean that when a professor has taught something for a long time, the information can get a little stale.

What students don't know about the job of faculty is just how much work goes into putting together a syllabus with a weekly breakdown of topics, readings, and what assignments/exams are best fit for the class. I also don't think they know just how hard it is to give someone an F at the doctoral level because of the potential impact on internship and beyond. I have lost sleep over this trying to double and triple check my scoring of assignments.

—Full professor, private PsyD program

Universities ask (or require) students to provide feedback on each course through some sort of evaluation. In some settings, student evaluations are important and taken very seriously; unfortunately, in other universities, they're an afterthought. No matter what, it's important that you complete them. Student evaluations can really help a professor hone the course and shape it for the next time it's offered. It's not the place to just complain (although you can do that too), but rather to offer some constructive feedback. Instead of just saying what didn't work, offer a suggestion about what might be even better. Remember, relationships are important in grad school, so be nice. Oh, and give your statistics and research methods professors a break. Those poor souls always have some of the worst evaluation scores because students are often not so enamored with the material. It's hard to teach that stuff, so pepper your evaluation with some encouragement!

On Professoring

The other (somewhat) hidden weight of being a professor is the interpersonal relationships between different professors in the department (i.e., politics). It's been said that academic politics are the worst kind of politics because the stakes are so small. Differences in clinical theory, pedagogical beliefs, or personal worldviews can cause substantial strife between faculty members. Of course, I think that the largest disagreements occur around funding and promotion issues. If your professors don't get along well, you're likely to know about it because you'll sense some of the tension. No matter what, your professors are invested in you and your success, so unless their squabbles get in the way of your progress, don't fret about it too much.

They don't seem to be dedicated to the students outside of their lab in a way I've experienced at other institutions. Also, there seems to be a lot of in-fighting among them, which is distressing.

—Second-year public PhD student

The other thing that faculty need to navigate is the relationship they have with administration (e.g., deans, provosts, presidents, chancellors, etc.). Most universities these days have "shared governance," which means that the faculty and administration share the running of the university. In some cases, there can be tensions and disagreements between faculty and administration on issues of money and resource allocation. Some faculty have unions to represent them as well. Again, none of this is likely to impact you much, but it can be an important aspect of what your professors deal with and what you might face if you decide to join our ranks.

One thing that has really stood out to me is the micromanaging and seemingly adversarial approach administration takes toward faculty. It's like we are on different teams and they need to be looking over our shoulders so we aren't being lazy or something. It feels pretty disrespectful in relation to the fantasy I previously held about heightened autonomy given that I'd arrived at the pinnacle of my training and education.

—Assistant professor, public MA program

So What Does Any of This Mean for You?

When I was a new faculty member at a research-oriented university, it was implied that my job was to crank out as many publications as I could in as little time as possible. As a new faculty member, I worked incessantly, often spending all weekend cooped up in my office with a coffeepot and SPSS. Luckily, I loved research and felt that my work was important. And even though many of us are primarily motivated to teach and mentor students, research productivity is the sine qua non for many tenure-track professors in PhD programs in larger universities. The treadmill toward tenure and promotion might mean that your professors are making choices about how and where to spend their time, and they might not be spending as much of their time on you or the classes you're taking.

When I became a professor, I was surprised at the general undervaluing of clinical training and expertise in academia.

—Assistant professor, public MA program

I think the hardest part of being a faculty member is juggling all the different responsibilities and commitments. I notice that faculty have a lot of pressure to publish or become tenured professors, and I can see that being really stressful.

—First-year public PhD student

My hope is that most professors in our field are dedicated and giving teachers, and I think that most of us take that job very seriously. Students also might not know how much time is needed to prepare for the first teaching of a given course (suffice it to say that if you're taking a course that a professor is teaching for the first time, he or she is working harder in that class than you are!). However, if a professor is pretenure (or secured employment), their first priority might be their research. If you are in a mentorship program where you work closely with one professor, that professor might really need your help to get things done. You can be a real hero by helping with literature searches, data analysis, or even just routine data entry (which is a total drag, but we've all done it). More than just being helpful to that faculty member, you're learning a lot about how to manage a research team, collaborate, and develop research skills that will help you for years to come. If you are expected to do research in that faculty member's lab, you might not have much freedom to choose which projects you work on or what research questions you can ask. Granted, that might be true for associate professors too, but they can often give you a little more wiggle room.

I still haven't fully come to terms with all the free labor that we have to provide before we are given a degree or career. The free labor isn't just time intensive, but also emotionally and mentally taxing.

—Second-year private PsyD student

I think it's OK for you to be curious with your professors about where they are in their careers and what their pressures are. Ask them. I urge you to have very frank and open conversations about what they expect of you, what kind of feedback you can expect, and what opportunities there might be for both you and your professors to advance in your careers. Remember, relationships are important.

Also, like I mentioned above, your professors are more adept at dealing with *academic time*, which is the glacial, red-tape-laden speed at which large entities operate. It's also the time of careful analysis and thoughtfulness. There are often multiple levels of oversight that can also eat into time. For example, if I incur an expense related to conference travel that the university plans to reimburse, it takes nearly two months for me to see that money. Likewise, if I propose a new class, there are at least *three* committees that review that course before I can offer it. Journals often take three months or longer to evaluate a manuscript (and I've had them take up to a year!). I often tell students that academic speed feels like tossing messages in bottles into the ocean: your stuff goes out, and there's often no feedback for a *very long time*. Get used to it, but also feel free to ask your professor about when you can expect to get responses to things or feedback on your work.

· · · · · · · · · · · · · · · · · **Words of Wisdom** · · · · · · · · · · · · · · · · ·

1. Get used to *academic time*.
2. Remember that your professors are people too.
3. Expect collegiality, but not warmth, from your professors. If you get warmth, that's a bonus.
4. Knowing your faculty's type and rank might make it easier for you to understand where they're coming from.

· ·

Professors Are People Too

When I was first hired as an assistant professor, one of my senior colleagues once said to me, "There's a big difference between students who understand that we're real people and those who don't." And she was right. When students remember that we're real human beings, with real lives, real growth trajectories, and real problems, issues, and limitations, the relationship can be more genuine, less "top down," and more collaborative. But if students see us only as "imposers of rules" or in loco parentis, then the relationship can have a sense of tension or resistance that can be relatively unpleasant.

And make no mistake, we are real people. In the time since I became a professor, I've gotten divorced, remarried, had a child, became a vegan, had some medical challenges, gotten a bunch of tattoos, started a private practice, grappled with depression, changed research and clinical specialties twice, and had more internal changes than I can describe. On those wonderful occasions when I can catch up with former students, it's always jarring to me to hear their questions about my life, because those questions are often about a me that I no longer am. People change. So do professors.

I bring all of this up to remind you that your professors are also on their own journeys. They're grappling with their own insecurities, developing as teachers, researchers, and mentors, and hopefully they have a shifting tapestry of experiences, relationships, and interests that are outside of their jobs. Some professors choose to be somewhat distant from their students, while some of us choose to wear our humanness on our sleeves. We all have strengths and weaknesses, and areas of vision and blindness, and the mere fact that we've been in academia for a long time means that we're likely to be a little weird. So if you're expecting perfect responsiveness, approachability, warmth, or consistency, you might be out of luck. However, we all have some degree of competence that has gotten us to where we are, so if you capitalize on our strengths (rather than being let down by our weaknesses), you'll have an easier journey.

I imagine it must feel really rewarding to see students move through the program, gain confidence in their skills, and find success.

—First-year public PhD student

Here's a few other things you can do to respect your professors' personness:

- Ask us how we're doing. And mean it.
- Don't expect us to read stuff over the weekend or after 5 p.m.
- Do things when you say that you will, or let us know that you need more time. It helps us plan our weekly workload.
- Be clear about what you want and need in an advisor and give your professor the benefit of the doubt. For example, I'm bad at imposing structure or timelines on my doctoral advisees, but if they ask for those things, I'm happy to implement them.
- Allow us to teach you. Nothing makes a professor happier than a student who is eager to learn.

Sail Your Mentorship

We all need mentors. Successful people will always point to mentors they've had as being instrumental in helping shape their professional careers. I have had a handful of really influential people in my life who have taken me under their wings. If it weren't for these caring, personal, and thoughtful mentors who pushed and pulled me and lent me wisdom, I'm not sure where I'd be. Even now, at the midpoint of my career, I seek out *wise elders* to help me think through my career, my teaching, my clinical work, and the balance of my personal and professional lives.

I actually work closely with three different faculty members. My original advisor is the person with whom I applied to work upon entering graduate school. He is a warm and supportive mentor, always encouraging me to reach my potential. I developed my second working relationship with a professor in a different department after taking one of his classes. He liked a hypothetical project I proposed in class and asked me whether I would be interested in working with him in a research capacity. He is a wonderful teaching mentor, challenging me to think critically about research questions and methods, providing me with new skills, and helping me develop my own academic identity. I sought out the relationship with my third mentor in yet another department because what she studies is directly in line with my research passions. If I had wanted a different degree, I would have likely applied to her lab. She provides me with the means and opportunity to research fascinating questions, as well as broadens my perspectives on the field I am in.

—Second-year public PhD student

A second year in my lab is my mentor. She has given me helpful advice and continues to answer my questions and provide guidance.

—First-year public PhD student

I have several mentors at graduate school; it is hard to pick just one. However, I would probably say my clinical supervisor. She has been a source of both personal and professional advice and has contributed to my growth as a clinical psychologist in a major way. I am very grateful to have had the opportunity to work with her.

—Second-year private PsyD student

I have a few people that I consider my mentor. These are mostly faculty and the relationships developed prior to graduate school when I worked as a research coordinator.

—First-year public PhD student

Some graduate programs are mentorship programs where you will work closely with one or two faculty members throughout your time in graduate school. Some programs will provide you with an advisor, but advising is different from mentorship, and some mentors in mentorship programs might not be good *mentors* for you. Find mentorship where you can. In your time in graduate school, you will meet professors and clinical supervisors you admire or who understand your worldview. I urge you to reach out to them, meet with them, and seek mentorship from them. My guess is that most will be happy and willing to give you pointers, suggestions, or wisdom along the way.

I identify as a gender, ethnic, and national-origin minority. I am also the first in my family to attend college. I think striking up close relationships with faculty and advisors who share similar minority identities or who can better relate to my struggles has made it easier to integrate into the field. Also, getting involved in research and partnering with researcher advisors that focus on ethnic minority/immigrant issues has been a wonderful way to learn more about similar populations I will be working with when I return to my home country.

—Reycine, second-year private PsyD student

I wish there were more Latina professors in my program that could mentor me. It would be great to be able to have someone who comes from a similar background as me and understands the struggles that minority students like myself encounter as doctoral students.

—Natalia, first-year public PhD student

I think that mentorship is particularly important for students from underrepresented groups, non-Western countries, or who are the first in their families to attend college or graduate school. Higher education can often bring out differences in backgrounds, and students of color or those from working-class backgrounds can feel alone with their worldviews. A number of organizations provide for the mentorship of diverse students,[2] and I urge those of you from underrepresented groups to reach out to psychologist mentors who have gone before you on how they have navigated the system and integrated their culture(s) of origin with the cultures of psychology.

Power

Obviously, as a graduate student, you are in a one-down power position relative to your faculty. Even the best mentorship relationship has a power and status difference. That often leaves students struggling with what to say and what to ask for and wondering how they're being perceived. Some impression management is warranted given that your faculty are the gatekeepers for your degree. And even as I note above that it's important to recognize your faculty's humanness, this is not an invitation to get too friendly or that you should expect them to be warm and caring.

[2] See http://www.apa.org/education/grad/mentor-task-force.aspx.

Sometimes it is difficult to draw the line between the personal and the professional. I am still navigating those boundaries.

—Second-year private PsyD student

The power differential can be difficult to navigate, particularly in mentorship-model programs where you're yoked to one professor for all of your research and advising (and sometimes clinical) needs. One of my colleagues once referred to mentorship-model programs as being "a setup for a bad marriage." Although you might jibe with a professor's research interests, you might not mesh with them personally. This might leave you feeling pretty alone and without guidance that feels personal or caring. I wish there was something I could offer to help you navigate that, but my advice is to expect a collegial but distant working relationship with your professors. It seems somewhat ironic given that your faculty are trained in *psychology*, but they might not ask much about your personal well-being, emotional wellness, or relationship status unless it impacts your productivity. That might feel like a loss to you if you've had close relationships with professors in the past, but it's best to prepare yourself for a more businesslike connection with professors in grad school.

Remember, relationships are important, and how you're perceived by professors is vital. You lack power, but you'll need to find a way to balance sticking up for yourself and merely going along with what you've been asked. It's a tricky balance, and other students can give you hints on how to handle some of that with your particular professors. In *most* cases, the best course of action is to be up front about things. If you're going to miss a deadline, say something; if you need a paper extension, ask for it ahead of time. Again, in *most* cases, a sneaky or passive-aggressive approach to dealing with the power imbalance will not serve you well. Note that I said *most cases*; use your clinical judgment and do what you can to protect yourself if you find yourself dealing with faculty who are, for whatever reason, unreasonable at a given time.

There's a difference between relationships that are unsupportive or disappointing and those that are caustic or damaging; if things go really badly, there's often someone you can go to for help (e.g., department chair, director of clinical training, ombudsperson). Don't hesitate to reach out, and my advice is to reach out even before you think you need to. I've seen relationships between students and faculty get sour pretty quickly, so speak to someone you can trust and who you know will shoot straight.

· · · · · · · · · · · · · · · · · · · **Tips and Strategies** · · · · · · · · · · · · · · · · · ·

1. Find a mentor and don't be shy about asking for guidance.
2. Ask for help from faculty before you need it.
3. Find out who to go to for help and support if things go badly.
4. Have open and honest conversations with your faculty advisors about what they expect of you.

I'll say it again: I love my job. I hope that many of you will consider careers in academia, because it's a really good gig. The opportunity to be relatively self-directed, to devote your energy toward research that you find important and meaningful, and to educate brilliant students toward professionalism is a real gift. Like all jobs, there are downsides, and some of those downsides have implications for you as a student. As you form relationships with your faculty, you'll meet a variety of people—some helpful, some not. In all cases, remember that we're human, that we have something to teach you, and that we're motivated to help you succeed.

CHAPTER 3

The Good, the Bad, and the Ugly: Your Student Colleagues

One of the oddest shifts between undergrad and grad school is the difference in the relationships you'll have with your student colleagues. As an undergrad student, you've likely had different classes with different people throughout any given week or year. If you've gone to a larger university, you've probably also had large lecture classes with potentially hundreds of students in them. So many faces, so many classes, so much interaction.

Grad school is a different ballgame. Grad school cohorts typically range from 4 to 30 students, and it's likely that you'll take many (if not all) of your courses with the same folks in the same sequence. Same handful of people, day in and day out, for a few years. That's a lot of togetherness. And you don't get to *choose* these people. As one student once said to me, "I love my colleagues, but it would be nice to see some other faces from time to time." If you're a big fan of being anonymous and blending in, you've made the wrong life choice.

The upshot of all this is that you'll likely make lifelong friends (or at least respected colleagues). Nothing binds people together like mutual suffering! You'll share what you're learning (in lots of ways), spend hours together entering data into statistics software, cooperate on research and class projects, co-lead groups, share group supervision, and crash together in hotels at conferences. They'll come to your wedding(s) and snuggle your children (or puppies). They are, in fact, what you'll remember most about the whole grad school journey.

And all that togetherness can be a total drag. All of you will go through low points, and going through low points in the company of others can lead to short tempers, misplaced words, and less than ideal exchanges. Or, more likely, you'll have a polite but not so close relationship with many of your colleagues that feels generally supportive but not particularly deep. In all cases, there will be relationships to navigate and a lot of time to navigate them. Remember, in graduate school, relationships matter, so taking some time to think carefully about, and engage creatively with, your colleagues is bound to make your journey more rewarding.

Competition and Cooperation

I was an insufferable graduate student. I was competitive and insecure (those words are generally synonyms) and felt as though I had to prove something by being the *most* this or the *best* that. I could justify a lot of that by thinking I was just doing what I needed to do to further my career, but the insecurity part is likely closer to the truth. Although I think I was generally well tolerated by my colleagues, I believe that I missed an opportunity to get to know some smart and interesting people in a more genuine way.

You've probably had to be pretty competitive to get into graduate school, but it's time to put that aside—for the most part. That said, there are times in graduate school when you'll need to be in direct competition with your classmates. In many programs, there are prized practicum spots that only a few students can take advantage of. There will often be research assistant or teaching assistant spots that must be applied for. There might be grants or fellowships with serious financial implications where you'll be in competition with your classmates as well. And, of course, the competitiveness that comes with applying to the same predoctoral internships can be daunting and complex to navigate. All of these situations are a normal part of the process, and there might be some tensions (or at least some discomfort) between you and your classmates when these situations occur.

When competitive situations arise, you'll need to figure out how to deal with them. Often it makes sense to acknowledge them openly: "Looks like we're both applying to the same practicum site. That's weird and awkward." Or "We've both submitted applications for the same grant. I sure hope you don't get struck by lightning." OK, well, maybe the second example isn't great, but you see what I mean. In many cases, just saying something about tension helps to relieve it. This is not to say that you need to have a long and compli- cated discussion about your feelings on the matter, but a simple acknowledg- ment is probably worthwhile.

More frequent than competitive situations are opportunities for coop- eration. Share readings, share study materials, share research data, share textbooks[1] and course notes, share clinical insights, share thoughts about how to navigate wacko faculty, and share support. If lots of togetherness isn't your bag, that's OK, but look for ways to share and help your colleagues. All of you will be better for it, and it's likely that you'll receive a return on that investment.

They are the only people who know what you are going through. My close friends in my program provide unconditional support.

—Fourth-year public PhD student

---

[1] Except for my books. You should always buy your own copies of those (a few copies, in fact).

· · · · · · · · · · · · · · · · · · · **Words of Wisdom** · · · · · · · · · · · · · · · · · ·

1. Don't make your graduate student colleagues your entire social circle.
2. If there's tension between you and your graduate student colleagues, find a way to talk about it.
3. Leave competitiveness behind. You'll gain nothing from it other than irritated colleagues and professors.
4. Comparison is a happiness killer. Keep your eyes on your own prize.

· ·

Mom Loves You Best!

Although there are situations that involve overt competition between graduate students, there is often a more subtle form of competition that can happen among students in a program. In each research lab, practicum group, or classroom, there's a handful of students and a faculty member. No matter how much a faculty member might like and respect all students, you may feel at times as though the professor likes or respects the other students more than you. Simply put, you might not feel like the favorite.

As a faculty member, I have always had the utmost respect, love, and appreciation for all of my students, but it's clear that I've clicked with some of them more than others.[2] And many students can be understandably distressed when they feel as though they're not liked as much as other students (whether that perception is real or imagined is another matter). Indeed, I've had many students come to me who were distressed that their colleagues were seemingly treated better or seen more favorably than they were by a professor in our department. They expressed some degree of resentment and jealousy about that and worried that their careers might suffer accordingly. In some of those cases, the student's suspicions were correct insofar as their professor liked other students more, but, in other cases, it was a reflection of the student's insecurity and competitiveness.

If you find yourself feeling like the neglected kid or resentful of the attention and praise that your colleagues get that you don't, the first thing to do is check yourself. Are you expecting something unreasonable? Might you be imagining the whole thing due to a general sense of inferiority or imposter syndrome? Are you a pain in the neck? Do you feel that you have earned the attention and praise that your colleagues have? (Deadbeat lab members who don't pitch in when asked are rarely on the short list of go-to students.) Are there large personality, culture, or other differences between you and the professor? And finally, does it really matter? That is, even if you feel as though your colleagues are more liked than you, will that affect your career trajectory?

On the flip side, if you feel as though the professor or teacher really likes you, perhaps even more than your colleagues, there are important things to understand there too. How much have you performed or sacrificed *just* to earn

---

[2] Unsurprisingly, I've clicked more with students who have also seen me as a human being (see Chapter 2).

that praise? Does your need for approval or attention lead you to compromises that you'd rather not make? To what extent have you reached out to your colleagues to be helpful and supportive? Have you thrown anyone under the bus in order to curry favors? Be careful of the allure of the golden ring—Gollum taught us that.

In any case, these subtle and sometimes not-so-subtle differences in faculty treatment (real or imagined) might lead you to feel either subtly or overtly competitive with, or resentful toward, people who could be your best friends and allies. My advice is to think of any perceived favoritism as a function of the professor, not the student. That is, if there's a student who is more favored, you can interpret that as a brown-nosing or overachieving student, or you can think of it as a failure on the part of the professor to be fair. Blame the professor rather than castigating your colleagues or separating yourself due to resentment or awkwardness.

Navigating Differences

Unlike friends in the real world, you can't choose your graduate student colleagues, but you're locked in with them for (usually) about three years of classes and often practica and research labs. Again, some of those people will end up being lifelong friends, but you might need to navigate some significant differences in background or personal experience.

Survey data[3] indicate that the modal psychology graduate student is an able-bodied, childless, heterosexual, European American woman in her late 20s. Although I don't have data on this situation, my guess is that most students are not the first in their families to attend college, nor are they likely to come from working-class or impoverished backgrounds. Even though there are always interpersonal differences between people, if you have a strikingly different life story from the rest of your classmates, this can make for a more complicated experience and perhaps an even greater imposter syndrome.

There were six of us in my graduate school class, and I was the only man. It wasn't until then that I realized how important having other men around was to me. Although my colleagues were great people whom I really respected, I always had a feeling of distance based on our sex. Furthermore, having grown up in the rural South in a working-class family, I *still* feel out of place in some of the more rarified arenas of higher education. These experiences, of course, are minor compared to the differences in race, nationality, sexual orientation, ethnicity, age, or disability status that some of you will face.

It seems to me that the biggest challenges of being "different" are loneliness, misunderstanding, and carrying the weight of representation. When we are similar to others, we have the freedom to speak in a shorthand of sorts. Our language changes, we share common points of reference, and we often feel more at ease. It's easier to find commonality and to grow close with people who are similar to us. If those people are not in our graduate school cohort, we can be left feeling isolated and lonely. Our social exchanges are challenged with more self-monitoring. I've heard many students from underrepresented groups talk

[3] See https://www.appic.org/Match/MatchStatistics/ApplicantSurvey2016Part1.aspx.

about the feeling of being lonely, homesick, and set apart from their colleagues, higher education, and the field as a whole.

We tend to misunderstand people who are different from us. Indeed, some research indicates that we're less accurate in reading the facial expressions of people of different races or cultures (Elfenbein & Ambady, 2002). Linguistic differences, idioms, personal experiences, and the experience of prejudice and marginalization can lead to misunderstandings between colleagues, hurt feelings, or simple frustration at having to explain things. Of course, all of this can exacerbate feelings of loneliness and give your imposter syndrome a huge boost.

My classmates kept saying, "Get it on Amazon." In my country, we only know Amazon as a river. I was so confused!

—Bernard, predoctoral intern, public PhD student

Finally, students from marginalized groups are often put in the position of carrying the weight of representation by essentially serving as spokespeople for an entire class of human being. As one student said to me, "I'm sick of being the spokesperson for all Black people!" If you're different from your colleagues, you might feel compelled to speak up in class to share a different perspective, but that can also put you in the spokesperson position. It's not fair that it happens (nor is it accurate), but it does.

I think it's important to have frank and open conversations about diversity and differences, but these conversations must be respectful and entered into with a great deal of humility. As is true for a lot of formalized education, much of the learning happens in the hallways, during meals, and in exchanges with people who might be different from you. Anyone who is a graduate student occupies a place of power and privilege in society, so the responsibility to be both humble and curious is even greater.

Entering grad school in my mid-40s has been educational in many ways. What I've learned from being thrust into a group of 20-somethings is as valuable as what I've learned from my professors—some of whom are also younger than me.

—Sharon, predoctoral intern, private PsyD student

Gossip and the Telephone Game

When you were a kid, did you ever play the "telephone game"? You stand in a circle or a line, and the leader whispers something in the ear of the person next to them, who whispers it to the person next to them, and so on down the line. What starts off at the beginning of the line as "I like cupcakes" winds up as "I'm afraid of clowns" at the end. Misunderstanding adds to misunderstanding, and eventually things get more and more distorted. I often think that this is what the graduate school fishbowl is like. I never thought of it that way until I became a faculty member and students would come to me concerned or upset about a particular new departmental policy, but their understanding of that policy would be largely incorrect. They heard it from someone, who heard it from someone, who heard it from someone. That's how organizations work (and it's not just a graduate school thing).[4]

My advice is to be extremely wary of hearsay. If you hear that the program is doing something drastic, it's probably not true (academia is almost never drastic). When possible, seek out the source and ask directly. Students often feel as though there's a certain lack of transparency in their programs (and often that's true), so I can understand the desire for information. Just be careful of what you hear and try not to get too carried away about thirdhand information.

Speaking of thirdhand information, let's talk a little about gossip. I grew up in a really small town (around 5,000 folks) in the middle of nowhere. By the time I was in third grade, I knew all sorts of dirt on families in town (including my teachers and my friends' parents). Grad school is like the smallest of small towns, and there's a tendency for bored graduate students to chat about their classmates and the faculty. You can share strong feelings about faculty members, but don't gossip about your fellow graduate students. Gossip is rarely helpful and usually inaccurate, and I've seen classmates and cohorts really get torn apart by idle talk. All graduate students have enough stress and anxiety to deal with without the stress and anxiety of being talked about. Be a rumor killer.

The Anxiety Contagion

Although the DSM doesn't say so, anxiety is as contagious as the flu or the common cold. It tends to be contracted more easily among high-strung and neurotic folks who have a tendency toward perfectionism (the kinds who get into graduate schools). In tightly knit graduate school communities that often have little contact with the outside world, epidemics of anxiety often run rampant. In fact, the anxiety bug can sometimes be so powerful that folks who are not anxious will get anxious about the fact that they're not as anxious as everyone else. The whole thing is nasty.

When I am feeling overwhelmed, I keep my distance. I like my space and quiet time at certain moments.

— Natassia, second-year private PhD student

All of this means that you need to keep a mindful eye on your anxiety and the anxiety around you. When approaching a big milestone such as qualifying exams, internship applications, and so on, it's likely that cohort anxiety will rise. In those situations, you need to be clear about how you discharge and manage your own internal disquietude. Don't be hesitant to go into interpersonal lockdown to prevent yourself from getting too torqued. Reach out to family and

---

[4] To be fair, faculty play the telephone game too.

nonstudent friends to help give you a reality check. Learn to recognize when your classmates are going a little off the rails (and when you are!), and do what you can to protect yourself. There's no vaccine other than awareness.

I remember thinking that despite the odds, I had managed to end up in a group of people where I was suddenly the least neurotic!

—Fifth-year public PhD student

A Bunch of Apples

In most graduate programs you'll move through the first couple of years of class work with a cohort. You and 4–90 other people will enter school at the same time and move through relatively the same program for a while. Because the human mind likes to categorize things, it's often the case that your cohort will be characterized by the faculty or staff in some way: the "quiet group," the "complainy group," the "angry group," the "young group," and so forth. Being categorized this way is clearly a way to cut corners and is most certainly inaccurate.

As is true for most group dynamics, the loudest and most vocal contingent will often set the reputation for everyone else. I've seen students cringe when one of their colleagues spoke up to say, "We all think it's really unfair that . . ." If you happen to be a vocal person, be aware that your vocalness has implications for everyone else in the cohort. Choose your words carefully and be professional. Always speak for yourself and use "I statements" whenever possible.

If you're a quieter student and find that someone else in your cohort is speaking on your behalf (without your consent), then you have a few options. If the spokesperson is generally doing a good and respectful job, then consider jumping in to help out. Don't always be the quiet one waiting for someone else to take the lead in setting the tone for classes and meetings. However, if the spokesperson is making you cringe, you might want to gently ask him or her to try to be somewhat more diplomatic in how they approach things.

Navigating these sorts of interpersonal dynamics is an essential part of your training toward being a psychologist and a professional. If you end up in academia (like me), there will be lots of occasions when you need to manage assertiveness, soothe the feelings of others, and consider how the group is functioning. If you work in clinical practice, you still need to interact with other treatment providers, clients and their families, and work colleagues if you're in a hospital or clinic. Because group dynamics will always be somewhat weird, consider this an opportunity to develop a life skill.

Once I have a conflict with a student colleague that I believe is more indicative of negative qualities they possess that are deal breakers for me, I only speak to them when absolutely necessary.

—Second-year private PhD student

Expanding the Circle

Get to know people who aren't classmates. I say this like it's obvious or easy to do, but I recognize that it's neither easy nor obvious. Being a student forces you into a somewhat myopic way of dealing with yourself and people around you. You're focused on the next paper, next externship, or next unappreciated milestone (see Chapter 7), often without coming up to do fun stuff or engage with the world around you. That's bad. And it's not a great way to live a life. Studies of creative people suggest that creatives will go out of their way to surround themselves with different people who challenge their perspectives or offer something new. Hunkering down with psychology folks is unlikely to offer you a full range of challenge or perspective.

I try to spend some social time with my cohort every month or two. I've found that keeping my own separate friends outside of graduate school has allowed me to keep my life in perspective and not worry about the small stuff. Plus, it's refreshing to hang around people who are not stressed out on the weekend!

— Third-year private PhD student

I socialize with my colleagues more during school. During break, I'm more into my family and friends back home and what they're doing.

— Second-year private PhD student

At most universities, there will be lots of graduate programs, from chemistry to biology to political science to medicine. Those types of schools are good at organizing functions for graduate students. You can also go to most events for nontraditional students (given that you're at least marginally older than most undergrads). I suggest you seek those out and give them a try or two. I've often heard graduate students talk about how important and relieving it is for them to have friends in other departments. Many of the requirements are the same, but they have different departmental politics, different players, and different trajectories.

In the spirit of *expanding the circle*, think twice before you date someone in your cohort or even your program. There are matters of convenience that make that a nice arrangement as well as a shared perspective and experience. But remember that you're living in a fishbowl that's usually pretty small. If things go badly, you're stuck there (often for years), and that can be awkward for everyone. I knew someone who dated another person in her graduate school cohort, and after they broke up they were matched to the same predoctoral internship for an additional year of tension and awkwardness. Again, it can be a great arrangement, and the heart wants what it wants, but it's good to be cautious.

Comparison Is a Happiness Killer

Everyone comes to grad school for different reasons. Each of you brings something unique, has different goals, and will have a different life trajectory. Some of you will be professors like me, some will be clinicians, some will consult, some will write science fiction novels, some will work in policy, some will work for nonprofits, some will take time off to raise kids, some will work in tech, and some will open taco trucks and make more money than any of the rest of us. That's cool. And it means that everyone will have a different graduate school story.

But it's natural to compare yourself to the students around you. How do they have so many publications already? How did they get that practicum site? Is everyone struggling like I am? Am I working hard enough? Should I be on four different projects too? Is my wardrobe too shabby? Indeed, the question I often get from graduate students is "Should I be doing more?"

Talk to your actual colleagues. My first year I was so worried that everyone around me was Mary-Sue perfect graduate student who was publishing every quarter, going to 20 conferences, applying to (and winning) every fellowship in town, and all while maintaining great hair, a perfect body, and a 10/10 partner in attractiveness. Once I actually spoke to my colleagues, I realized that all of that was just my own insecurity doing a stellar job of freaking me out and reinforcing my imposter syndrome. We're all doing the best we can, and we do a better job dealing with our own insecurities if we're brave and just ask how everyone else is doing (chances are they're freaking out too).

—Second-year public PhD student

Things always look different from the outside than they really are. Yes, maybe your colleague has more publications than you do, but do you really need that many for your career objectives? Are they independently wealthy and unburdened with work or assistantship responsibilities? Do you have more clinical experience? Have you taken more classes? Did their advisor just hand them a data set? Have you had time to go water skiing? "Productivity" can be measured in lots of different ways, and only you can define what's productive for you. Don't get ensnared in someone else's goals.

If you feel that you're really falling behind, ask your colleagues about how they're doing what they're doing. Find out how they're going about their lives and where they're getting help with their projects. You might find out that some people are really compromised or that they're independently wealthy and they don't need to work to pay rent. Talk to your faculty advisor about your progress and accept that they're being honest and truthful. No matter what you discover, you do you. Keep your focus on the things you want and need, and the rest will fall into place.

How to Play Well With Others

It's important that you're a good graduate student colleague because it makes everyone's life a lot easier in school. Being a good citizen is vital and will make the whole graduate school experience a lot more manageable. Instead of trying to be the smartest, be the nicest and the most giving; that will get you further in the end than competition ever will.

Being dishonest, fake, competitive, and rude makes for a bad colleague.
—Fourth-year public PhD student

Being selfish makes you a bad student colleague.
—Second-year private PhD student

The qualities that make a good grad school colleague are the things that make a good citizen in any environment. Be complimentary, polite, eager to help, and giving with your time and resources. Being too competitive is a real turnoff and is likely to isolate you in a hurry. If you think of your relationships as only lasting for the time you're in school, you're missing an opportunity. At least some of your student colleagues are likely to end up being professional colleagues at some point, so being weird or off putting now can potentially make a relationship awkward for years to come. Be nice. Your mom would want you to.

· · · · · · · · · · · · · · · · · **Tips and Strategies** · · · · · · · · · · · · · · · · ·

1. Find ways to cooperate and be generous.
2. Be open and respectful about diversity. Share and ask questions with humility and respect.
3. Don't gossip.
4. Don't always be the first or last to speak.
5. Be nice to your colleagues; they'll probably end up being some of the best friends you'll ever have.

· ·

You didn't start this journey alone, and you won't end it alone, either. Your student colleagues are your best allies and potentially your best friends. Although you don't get to choose these people, your lives will be drawn together for a pretty lengthy journey. Be a good colleague, share the ups and downs, and look forward to forging relationships that can last a lifetime.

Reference

Elfenbein, H. A., & Ambady, N. (2002). On the universality and cultural specificity of emotion recognition: A meta-analysis. *Psychological Bulletin, 128,* 203–235.

CHAPTER 4

Research Is Me-Search

When I was an undergraduate, I worked as a research assistant for a professor in our department. I was in charge of entering data and running preliminary analyses in statistical software. For the most part, the work was a drag; it was boring and relatively repetitive, but it was better than the other job I had in the cafeteria dish room. One day, however, my professor looked at some piece of statistics output, and we talked about what the finding meant. At some point in the discussion, she said simply, "This is really going to help a lot of people." In that one sentence, she connected the long hours of data entry that I was doing with a bunch of statistical gobbledygook to arrive at a finding that actually *meant* something . . . to *people*. At that moment, I finally realized the value of psychological research.

From that time forward, I built a career around using research as a way of learning and knowing things (and securing tenure; see Chapter 2). Not every project I've done has been rewarding and meaningful (most of them haven't been), but some of them have really been exciting and fun to do and, more important, have contributed knowledge that hopefully *helps people*. I say all of this because I often find that students think of research as being (a) intimidating and/or (b) boring. Both of those things certainly can be true (and will be if you do it enough), but I think that if you approach research work as a way to solve a mystery or really discover something new and interesting, it will be a lot more compelling. And if you're a student who is really excited and energized by research (either producing or reading), I hope that you can keep that spark alive because our field needs you.

Just think—as a student, you have the opportunity to make a discovery or learn something that no one else knows. Even if that discovery is very "small" or only contributes to a narrow band of inquiry (as most research does), it is still a useful contribution. You have contributed or organized information that will inform future research, future research designs, or clinicians and policy makers who are at the front lines of helping others.

The best part of research for me is passing it along. I use a lot of research sound bites in my clinical work, and it drives home a lot of messages that otherwise clients wouldn't be receptive to. Discovery is an amazing process, but putting that research to good use is really satisfying.

—Fifth-year public PhD student

Oftentimes, the most frequent use of research in the process of therapy is when I cite findings about a topic that the client asks about during a session. For example, a client I saw today asked about heavy marijuana use during adolescence. I happened to have written a paper about that last year, so I told her about the findings. Other uses of research include doing my best to inform my practice with evidence-based findings. I want to use what has been shown to work well, although I sometimes find it hard to transform the research into practice. Work still needs to be done around that area.

—Josh, fourth-year public PhD student

The Science of Psychology

Although our brothers and sisters in the natural sciences might disagree, psychology is a science. That is, the field of psychology values the scientific method as a means of *knowing*. Clearly, there are other ways of knowing (or thinking you know) things to be true (e.g., religion, personal experience, hearsay), but psychology looks to the methods of science to confirm or disconfirm hypotheses. When done well, this process leads to important expansions of knowledge and a deeper understanding of psychological and social phenomena.

Although psychology is a science, it is an *inexact* one. Our methods are error prone, our methodology often involves arbitrary decisions, and our subjects (human beings) are highly variable. Indeed, a recent large-scale study found that many classic findings in psychology have failed to replicate (Open Science Collaboration, 2015). We might be a science, but we're a messy one.

What this might mean for you is that you need to deal with a lot of research-related frustration to go along with your research-related excitement. Coping with all the limitations of our research, all the decisions, and all the pragmatics can be a real drag. And your meetings with your research advisor might get frustrating when it comes time to actually design a study. Indeed, each year, I have a few research talks with students that I call "research dream killers." In those meetings, a student comes to my office excited with a well-considered project idea that I then systematically destroy with questions about threats to validity, prior research, or simple financial and/or time barriers. In the best-case scenario, we come up with a revised project that's doable, answers a good question, and will contribute to the literature. But that doesn't always happen, and often a student must sit with some substantial frustration.

I didn't think I was going to be a researcher (and to be fair, I mostly focus on clinical work), but I enjoy the process of fitting a design to a research question.

I've had to downsize a lot of my ideas from when I entered grad school, now that I know more about feasibility. I most enjoy seeing research at work with community and governmental organizations. It's quite rewarding.

—Fifth-year public PhD student

I really like conducting clinical research and feel like doing that kind of work is really beneficial for my own understanding of the therapy process, and in a broad sense how I see and approach doing therapy myself. I also find it frustrating for a number of reasons, mostly because the language and process can be very esoteric and complicated, and it draws on skills that don't all come that naturally to me. So it's a mixed bag, but I find it mostly gratifying.

—Seth, predoctoral intern, private PhD student

The other way that the science of psychology impacts you is that you'll be expected to think scientifically. Sophisticated scientific thinking is a form of skepticism that relies heavily on evidence in decision making and reasoning. Likewise, scientific thinking is a way of thinking that recognizes the limitations of what we know and how we know it. To practice scientific thinking, be quick to do literature searches on topics of interest to you or that are related to your clients' functioning. Read literature with a skeptical eye to clearly articulate what we can reasonably learn from a given article and what questions remain. Finally, recognize that what you might think is true based on your experience or what seems to be true may not be true for all people (or true at all). Be humble in what you think you know, and open your mind to being corrected and assimilating new knowledge.

Research is one of the things that differentiate clinical psychologists from other disciplines that also allow one to do therapy. Early on in grad school, my mentor encouraged me to strive to think like a psychologist, rather than (or in addition to) a therapist. There's nothing at all wrong if research isn't your thing, but if you choose to dismiss it, I think it's important to be aware that you may be missing out on the opportunity to increase your knowledge in ways that may be important to you (without your even realizing it).

—Seth, predoctoral intern, private PhD student

Research training is one of the most important aspects of training; otherwise it's difficult to know if you're being duped or well informed. But research training also teaches you how difficult it is to get a clear answer to some questions, and the limits of science in explaining human behavior.

—Fifth-year public PhD student

1. Research is a process of solving mysteries!
2. A null finding is still a finding. No matter what you find, you've still learned something.
3. When learning statistics, it's helpful to understand the concepts before you start to deal with the math or the statistics output.
4. Publication is not as hard as you think it is (but it might test your resilience).

· ·

N = 1: You and Statistics

STATISTICS! The HORROR! No single word strikes fear into the hearts of (many) graduate students like *statistics*. Many of us drifted into the social sciences and humanities because we enjoyed the fact that those fields are about humans rather than complicated mathematics procedures and formulas that seem disconnected from reality. I don't know about you, but I'd rather have a debate about the nature of humanity than spend hours digging through a set of math proofs (although, to be fair, I really like statistics). My guess is that it's those personal preferences, and maybe even general math-related anxiety, that make statistics such a sticking point for so many students. In my experience, the anxiety is generally overblown, but it all depends on your relationship to mathematics in general, the quality of your statistics instructors, and your ability to understand abstract concepts. Most students seem pleasantly surprised when statistics doesn't turn out to be the monster they fear it will be.

It seems that most graduate programs require at least a year of statistics. Some PhD programs require more; some PsyD and MA programs require a lot less. No matter what, you'll need to learn how to make some sense of new vocabulary and how to find stuff in SPSS.

Statistics classes were a lot of work, yet also useful. I tried to get the fundamentals down, despite poor-quality teaching of the intro stats course. I also found that if I didn't use it, I'd lose it. So trying to play with various analyses with more frequency helped keep it fresh.

—Fifth-year public PhD student

The simplest advice I give to students taking statistics is that they really need to understand the material *conceptually*. As a psychology student, you're already a good conceptual thinker, so take advantage of your strengths. If you get lost in the mathematics and threats to validity, it's easy to get overwhelmed. I was lucky enough in graduate school to have a good stats professor, but, like many stats professors, he could get a little lost in his head and the esoterica of formulas. Despite his wisdom and experience, I felt pretty lost in the beginning. But eventually I realized that I needed to take a step back and see the larger, conceptual picture in what he was teaching me. Also, I'm a visual learner, so once I could picture *t* tests as two overlapping normal curves and correlations as a couple of scatter plots, the ideas of *variance, standard deviation,* and *regression* made a lot more sense to me.

No matter how you approach it, make peace with statistics, and if you have stats anxiety, figure out whether that anxiety is warranted. And if you really struggle, don't hesitate to get a tutor. No matter what, if you're sharp enough to get into graduate school, you're bright enough to get through statistics. If you're like me and you find it fun, enjoy a really fun way of answering interesting questions!

If you want to be good at it, there's really no way around putting in the hours. There are a lot of skills and concepts involved, and you have to actually spend time doing the work yourself; otherwise, you'll always be relying on others, which will ultimately be constraining.

—Seth, predoctoral intern, private PhD student

Beyond mere tolerance of anxiety, I urge you to try to *enjoy* statistics. All data are a hidden story, and stats allow you to uncover that story. With many of my students over the years, I've had "data parties" when we have used a projector to put the data up on the wall so that we can run the statistics together and share in the process of discovery. In the entire research process, I love the data analysis phase the most. Once you get the hang of it, statistical analysis of the data becomes a language that you can speak with some degree of fluidity, and it can help you reveal things that no one has ever known before. And, more important, those things can really help people.

Dissertation

No matter what kind of program you're in, you'll probably need to write some sort of capstone paper (sometimes more than one). Dissertations and/or theses are required by most universities and really do represent the culmination of your graduate education. Many of these projects will take you a year or more to complete and will be held to a very high standard. Daunting, yes, but it's also an opportunity to dive deeply into a topic that's of interest to you.

Dissertations can take many forms, and your university will have guidelines about what kinds are allowable. Some universities require an empirical dissertation that involves statistics and data analysis or qualitative analysis. Some will allow you to use archival data (that you didn't collect), but some will require you to collect your own data. Many PsyD programs will allow you to do a systematic literature review or a case study (which sounds like it would be easy, but it's not). The type of dissertation or thesis you choose to do will have substantial implications for how you spend your time, so, if given the choice, choose carefully.

Regardless of the type of dissertation or thesis you write, there will generally be a few formalized steps. First, you and your chair will come up with a dissertation project idea, and you'll write a formal proposal about how you'd like to conduct your study. The proposal document will generally include a synthesis of the research along with a specific methodological approach (including participant recruitment, sample size, measures, etc.). Once that proposal is in good shape, you'll have a meeting with your dissertation or thesis committee where you'll pitch the idea to them. In my experience, dissertation proposal meetings are collegial and relaxed affairs where the student and the committee work together to agree upon an acceptable project. When all goes well, you'll leave the meeting feeling like you have a clear project to work on and that you and your committee have a workable contract.

After you've collected data, run the stats, and written the results and discussion sections of your paper, you'll have a defense meeting. Your chair will let you know when you're ready to defend, and you and your committee will come together again to hash out the results. In most universities, these are open to the public, so you might be presenting to an audience. Unlike a proposal, the defense can be a lot more challenging. Although it's likely that most faculty will be supportive and helpful, some can be outright adversarial or take it as an opportunity to grill you. I think this is pretty rare, and it usually signals that there's a strained relationship between two faculty members on your committee rather than there being something objectively wrong with your project—you're merely getting caught in the crossfire. However, most proceed pretty smoothly and allow students to show off their expertise, competence, and facility with the material. In many cases, students will need to make some revisions afterward, but, in my experience, we've never failed a student or asked them to redefend. Once you've made it to the defense, you're probably in pretty good shape and the finish line is just at the top of the hill.

My biggest concern was that I would be asked a question and not know it. Practicing a few phrases for how to handle that situation really put my mind at ease. Once the presentation started, though, I realized I was just sharing info on a subject I knew quite a bit about, and the words just came naturally. I may have still felt nervous/excited, but I also felt assured nothing disastrous was going to happen.

—Fifth-year public PhD student

Of course, the first step in a dissertation or thesis is forming a committee. The chair of the committee will likely be your major advisor or someone else whose research interests match your own. You'll need to assemble a committee of one to three other faculty who will lend their expertise to your project. Depending on the work you're doing, committee members can help you with various components of the work, provide you with resources, or offer feedback on drafts. To the extent possible, it's important to form a committee of faculty with whom you have a good working relationship and who you know will be fair with you. I've heard rumors of faculty members being completely ruthless with students so that they are no longer asked to be on student committees; other students in your department will let you know who is good to work with and whom to avoid.

There are countless books and manuals on writing dissertations, so I won't offer those sorts of pragmatics here. But here are a few tips:

1. The most important quality of a dissertation is that you can complete it in a reasonable time. Sophistication, statistical complexity, and comprehensiveness of coverage don't mean much when you're entering your 12th year of graduate study. Make sure it's doable in the time you have.
2. Do something you're passionate about. It's too long of a road to do a project that doesn't turn your knobs, so you should be interested in the topic area. At some point, you'll get tired of the whole thing, so having some passion to propel you along will make a huge difference. No matter what, remember how your work has the potential to help people. However, you should always remember the first rule (do a project that you can complete), so if your ultimate passion is to do a longitudinal study of left-handed birdwatchers, maybe save that until you're a faculty member.

I had hoped my dissertation would be in an area of stronger interest than it was, but I still found it intriguing enough that it wasn't a headache to sit down hours each day and put words on the paper. Sure, it was tedious and I felt socially isolated many days, but the actual subject matter was of strong enough interest that I was often curious to find out more. If the process seemed like a drag at times, I reminded myself that we have the internet and that previous academics would use a typewriter and spend days in the library hauling around loads of books.

—Fifth-year public PhD student

---

3. It's not one big paper; it's lots of little papers! One thing that helped me write my dissertation was that I thought of it as lots of little papers (probably 15 or so of them). Once I had a solid outline, I just picked a section, did the legwork, and wrote it. The introduction and discussion sections are particularly amenable to sectioning. By now, you're good at writing papers, so if you break the project up into manageable pieces, it'll help keep moving you forward.
4. Deadlines are your friends. Even if you're the most self-motivated student in the world, you could still use some external reinforcers and motivators. If your dissertation chair doesn't impose deadlines, gently ask to have some imposed upon you. If that's not feasible, give yourself deadlines for each section. I've seen many students get lost in the process because there weren't enough deadlines or enough structure.
5. Do everything in your power to complete your dissertation (or most of it) before you start your predoctoral internship. I can't emphasize this enough. Your year of full-time clinical training is precious time, and it's stressful time when you'll be stretched to your limits in a lot of ways. Having to come home after a full day of clinical training and try to remember where you were on your dissertation project is a real nightmare. In my internship

class, you could look around the room and tell who had defended their dissertations and who hadn't; those with incomplete dissertations looked underslept, stressed, and depressed. Also, remember that if you've completed your dissertation prior to internship, you can use that internship year to get involved with new projects that might lead to postdocs, faculty positions, and other opportunities. Make that internship year as good as it can be.

6. Pick a short title. This sounds like a minor thing, but your dissertation title travels with you for the rest of your career. Particularly for those of you who want careers in academia, you'll need to regurgitate your dissertation title on various forms and documents forever. You'll need to write it when you apply for licensure, and many people include it on their vitae. If your title is 37 words long, you'll need to drag all 37 words out more often than you think.

7. Make friends with H_0. Many (if not most) research projects will yield null results. We test stuff, and that stuff doesn't come out the way we expect it to. In the natural sciences, a null result may result in a revision of the study, or the researcher might shrug and try something different, having learned that the initial hypothesis was incorrect. But in our field, particularly when students work for a year on a dissertation project that yields a null result (or several), they often feel really disappointed and as though the project was a failure. Not so. Although we like to find results that support our assumptions, when we fail to reject the null hypothesis, we still *learned* something. Null results add just as much value to our understanding of something as a significant finding. Be proud of H_0.

Publishing Without Perishing

If you're a doctoral student, I highly encourage you to try to publish while you're in graduate school. For those of you in PhD programs, you might be required to submit research for publication, and even if you aren't required, it's an important and useful process that might pay you back in the future. For those of you in PsyD programs that might not have many research requirements, I'd still urge you to be on the lookout for opportunities to publish.

The benefits to getting something in print are numerous. If you're headed toward a career in academia (particularly in a research university), you'll need as many publications as you can get. (I often say that publications in academia are like cigarettes in prison: they act as a form of currency that can buy you a lot of neat stuff.) But even if you're headed for a career in practice or in a teaching-oriented academic position, there are still benefits to publication. First, you'll contribute to knowledge! Even if you don't intend to take the work further, your work will still be useful to others who are working in the field. Second, it might help you get an internship. Although publications aren't needed or even heavily prized by internship directors, a publication or two will help you stand out a bit in the pile of applicants. Postinternship jobs often like to see some variance in your vitae as well. Third, it will give you some appreciation for the process of publication and the quality of peer review so that you can be an even more informed consumer of research. Finally, it's fun! (At least in a nerdy way.) To finally get an acceptance and see your name in print is a real treat, no matter how many times you've done it.

I have not published anything yet, which feels like a failure, especially coming from a PhD program. To handle this reality, I consider life factors (health and relationship issues) that were prioritized and affected my ability to juggle the demands of grad school. I also try to focus on current opportunities to make a publication happen. I feel a bit of disappointment in not taking advantage of the many opportunities I had, or seeking more out during my schooling, but in the end there are only so many hours in a day, and one only has so much energy.

—Fifth-year public PhD student

So what can be published? Obviously, research papers with original data are nearly sure bets. But consider expanding on the papers you write for class as possible candidates for publication. There are a number of journals that specialize in review papers where a well-written conceptual paper can find a home. Often overlooked are papers that translate bodies of research into clinician-friendly summaries. These "science-to-practice" papers are much needed and can often be derived from class projects. And not all papers need be long tomes with complicated statistics and endless reams of references; a small but well-designed study will find a home in print just as easily (if not more so).

If you've never done it before, the publication process can feel intimidating. The idea of sending your work out to be reviewed by anonymous strangers is daunting and can result in some serious blows to the ego. Although potentially intimidating, the publication process is relatively straightforward. First, you'll pick a journal that seems like a good outlet for your work (pro tip: scan your references section for the journal that you've cited most and consider submitting there first). Then you'll submit your paper through the journal's website along with a nice cover letter describing why the study is important. The journal editor will then make an initial determination of whether the paper is appropriate for the journal. If so, he or she will send the paper off to two or three reviewers. Almost all reviews are double-blind, meaning that the reviewers won't know who you are and you won't know who they are. Those reviewers will read your paper and send comments along to the journal editor; usually this part takes as long as three months. Comments from reviewers will range from critiques on your design and/or conceptual understanding to nitpicky grammar notes. From those reviews, the journal editor will make a determination to accept, reject, revise and resubmit, or accept with revisions. I tell students that they should expect to get rejected from the first journal they choose (and maybe the second and third too!). But with each submission to a different journal, the paper will get stronger and the work that emerges in the end will be a better product than the original.

The first time that students get reviewers' comments, it can be a real shock. Expect a page or two of comments from each reviewer, and, as might be expected, nearly all of those comments will be negative or critical. It's the job of a reviewer to break a study down so that only quality work is published. But if you can think of it as *constructive* rather than merely *critical*, it'll feel a little better (a *little* better). Every paper I've ever published has been made better through the review process, and the anonymous reviewers have been instrumental in increasing the quality of my work.

Tips and Strategies

1. Continue to develop your scientific thinking skills. Be critical, challenge your assumptions, and seek evidence.
2. Get a stats tutor if you struggle even a little bit.
3. The most important quality of a dissertation is that you can finish it. Do your dream study later.
4. Be quick to do literature searches on things of interest to you or questions that might arise during classes or meetings with clients.

No matter how you feel about research—doing it, reading it, or using it—it's arguably the most important asset of our field. By investigating our hunches and refining our theories, we produce knowledge that *helps people*. We ensure the public trust by grounding our work in evidence (and grounding our research in practice). Although it might just seem like spinning wheels at times, a scientific mind and academic skepticism are vital tools of the trade. As a student, you have much to contribute both in the production of that knowledge and in its translation to your work with clients.

Reference

Open Science Collaboration. (2015). Estimating the reproducibility of psychological science. *Science, 349*, aac4716. http://dx.doi.org/10.1126/science.aac4716

CHAPTER 5

Approaching Clinical Work

For many of you, clinical training is the most important part of your journey toward being a psychologist. It's the part of your training that feels special, different, and exciting (and not like school in the traditional sense). As you approach this part of the journey, you're likely excited, nervous, and completely unsure what to do.

By far, the most rewarding and important part of my job is serving as the supervisor for beginning graduate students. As students anxiously await their first client and welcome them into the therapy room, the energy is wonderful and fresh. No matter what the outcome of that first 50-minute hour, the student is changed forever: they're a therapist! It's still exciting for me to witness, and I've been honored to be a part of that journey for many student clinicians. My hope is that, if you're inclined toward practice, clinical work never loses that sense of newness and wonder for any of you.

But although it's an exciting process, it can be a stressful one. I can clearly recall the moment, now 20 years ago, that I went in and sat down with my first psychotherapy client. And as I closed the door of the therapy room, I thought, *I have absolutely no clue what I'm doing.* Luckily, my client had plenty on his mind, so I was able to surf through that first session with little more than some *uh huhs* and a few *that's interestings.* Afterward, as I sat down to write the process note, I realized that I'd been so anxious during the session that I couldn't quite recall what we'd discussed. It was a rough start to an aspect of my professional life that has brought me much meaning and joy over the past two decades.

I wish I had called a therapist I admired, like one of my professors, and asked them to share what they remember about seeing their first patient, hearing advice they may have had, or what they would have done differently in their early experiences becoming a therapist. When it comes to learning how to do clinical work for the first time, I have learned the most from mentor relationships.

—Third-year private PsyD student

The most challenging part about clinical work so far has been my own anxieties about doing it "wrong" or coming across as if I have no idea what I'm doing (which, let's be honest, sometimes I really don't). However, with more face-to-face hours, that anxiety starts to subside, and my confidence in the room builds. With the anxiety out of the way, I feel like I can be more present and focus on my client's needs.

—Fourth-year PhD student

All of this is a reminder that nothing can adequately prepare you for your first session and, no matter what, you'll get better at it (without ever feeling a sense of mastery).

Walking into a therapy room for the first time as a therapist felt a little like I was a little kid playing dress up in grownup clothes and trying to walk in oversized high heels. I had no idea what I was doing and felt like a total fraud of a therapist. I don't think it's possible to really prepare for that moment, for that first patient. It wasn't until I looked at that man sitting across from me and saw his fear matching mine that I realized he was nervous too. Starting therapy can be daunting. So, I took a deep breath and started getting to know him. The best preparation I had for that moment didn't come from a book or a lecture but a fleeting comment from a colleague who had just seen her first patient: "My only goal is to not run out of the room in panic."

—Nicole, third-year private PsyD student

In my very first session as a clinician, I had no idea what I was doing. I had been taught about reflective listening, but I felt that I had no clue how to actually guide my client in a therapeutic way. I felt like my client may be able to detect that I was lost, and this scared me. I worried about wasting my client's time and money.

—Natalie, third-year private PsyD student

Each time I supervise a group of practicum students, someone will invariably confess to me that they don't feel prepared for their first session. My response is "Of course you don't!" You've never done it before, people are unpredictable, and the whole enterprise of therapy is a complicated mixture of science, experience, and art. Even if you've read all the books and watched all the videos, you won't be prepared. It's scary, and I always wish that I could help students feel more secure with their first client. Although nothing can prepare you fully for that first session, as someone who has supervised a number of students through their first rocky therapeutic encounters, I have a few words of advice for your first hour:

1. Don't try to accomplish anything. As a student, you'll read about treatments that emphasize homework assignments or perfect interventions that will bring about flashes of insight that will clarify everything. As a new clinician, it can be tempting to think you need to barrel into a session and magically change someone's life. Surely a *good* therapist would do that, right? Probably not. Years ago, I had a supervisee who proudly told me that he had given his client *four* homework assignments in their first meeting. We never saw that client again.

   Never underestimate the effectiveness and power of being a good listener. Clients come to therapy with a story to tell. In that first session, just be curious about their story, what brings them in, what they want, and what they fear. Just sit with them, gather a little information, connect, and hear where they're coming from. You'll accomplish more than you think you will.

   Clinical work is slower than I expected it to be. It is easy to get ahead of where patients are at and try to rush change or vulnerability. So much of what I end up doing in practice is slower than I planned if I'm listening to my patient well.

   —Nicole, third-year private PsyD student

   I honestly didn't know exactly what to expect at first. There are classic therapist tropes that we see in movies and read in books, and I guess that's all I had to go on. I suppose I thought that it would be a clearer process and that if I just read some books and had some good mentors, it would be relatively straightforward. I have since learned that therapy is a very complicated process sometimes, and other times it's just helping someone make a decision about which college offer to accept. The topics are so broad and varied that it is difficult to predict what will happen in any given session with any given client.

   —Josh, fourth-year public PhD student

   ---

2. Reduce paperwork fumbling. In nearly all clinics, there's a lot of paperwork to do in the first meeting: consent forms, video-recording forms, parking issues, and fees. Know what's in that paperwork before you hand it over to the client to deal with. It sounds like a small thing, but if you're clear with your paperwork, it'll help you and the client feel more like you know what's going on (even if you don't). Likewise, if you're doing a structured or semistructured intake session, know those questions, how to ask them, and what the general sequence will be.

   I tend to be someone who gets bogged down by little logistical issues until they become muscle memory. The most stressful part of seeing my first client was printing the release forms and clinic policy forms, making sure I had a clipboard/

pen for the patient to sign, having my own notepad and paper, making sure my key worked to the therapy room (also—does the room have a panic button/phone that works?), making sure I had a timer/clock and tissues, and that I knew how to work my video camera/memory card and could plug it in. The image I had of a therapist is a well lived-in office, but as a trainee at a busy clinic, I am often moving from room to room at each hour.

—Third-year private PsyD student

3. Remember ethics. Most of you will have a course in ethics prior to starting psychotherapy. Prior to your first session, refamiliarize yourself with limits of confidentiality, duty to protect and warn, and informed consent. More important, be comfortable with your setting's processes and procedures for making reports, dealing with emergencies, and consultation processes. Having a solid grasp of ethics and legal processes prior to walking into the unknown might serve you well and help you feel more confident and secure.

4. Know as much about your client as you can. If your clinic has a separate intake versus therapy process, study the intake notes. If you can, talk to the intake clinician about his or her impressions of the client (although take those impressions with a grain of salt). Remember details about the client, their presenting problems, and their life details. Knowing this information will help prepare you, but it will also make the client feel as though they don't need to repeat themselves.

5. It'll probably go more smoothly than you think it will. Ostensibly, you're in this field because, at least on some level, you're interested in people. You might not be *good* with people, but you're probably interested. If you can give voice to your interest in this person sitting with you, you'll be off to a good start. In my experience, the two questions that new clinicians often fear the most—"Have you worked with someone like me before?" and "How old are you anyway?"—rarely come up (at least in the first session). Both you and the client are trying to make a good impression, and that is enough to smooth out a lot of the rough spots.

6. Have fun! Starting clinical work is an important rite of passage. Enjoy it! It's true that you're flying blind and unlikely to solve all of someone's problems in the first 50 minutes, but if you can find a way to appreciate the opportunity to share in someone's life, to feel the trust of someone in a vulnerable position, and to honor the experience of being a helpful figure, your first session can be a rich and powerful experience.

The biggest surprise for me about beginning clinical work was how much I loved it. Of course, I had done a bunch of research and soul-searching before I went into this field, but prior "clinical-ish" experiences (i.e., crisis hotline counseling, etc.) hadn't prepared me for how exhilarating and interesting the therapy hour was and how rich the process of building an alliance is, which begins from the first moment.

—Third-year private PsyD student

. . . . **Words of Wisdom** . . . .

1. No matter what, you won't feel prepared to see your first client.
2. Your first goal should be to listen . . . to your clients, to your supervisor, to your colleagues, and to your gut.
3. Use supervision to help with challenges in the therapy, not just to show off what you can do.
4. It's OK to feel inadequate or that you can't help as much as you'd like to.
5. Remember that psychotherapy is a craft, composed of research, experience, and the needs of the clients.

. . . .

Swimming With a Life Preserver: How to Be Supervised

In the same way that you've not been a therapist before, you've never been a supervisee before. Like the therapeutic relationship, the supervisory relationship is a central component of therapy. I've had more supervisors than I can remember. Some of them I liked; some of them I didn't. But no matter what, I learned something from each one (even if what I learned is that their style of therapy didn't suit me). Like therapy, it might be hard to know what to expect of supervision and what will be required of you.

First, it's important to be prepared. A few years ago, a new supervisee brought me a printed agenda on letterhead that outlined her long-term objectives and short-term goals for each of her clients. That was overkill, but I appreciated the sentiment. Good preparation means having a few things that you'd like to cover, a few rough spots that you'd like to address, and some reflectiveness about what you might have done differently. Bringing those things to the attention of your supervisor will help you both stay on track and lead to better patient care.

I will never have more supervision per hour of clinical work than I had my first year as a trainee, and it was not enough. In an hour of (individual) supervision per week it sometimes feels like I barely scratch the surface of what has been going on in my clinical work.

—Third-year private PsyD student

Make peace with the feeling of insecurity. In many places, you'll video record your sessions and watch parts of those videos with your supervisor. This will make you feel incredibly vulnerable at first, but you'll get somewhat more comfortable with it. You'll be watched by someone who has more experience and wisdom than you do. Although it can make you feel *judged*, I can tell you that, as a supervisor, my thoughts are not on negatively evaluating the student's performance, but rather on helping them improve and how best to understand the client. You will get more comfortable being on video, and hopefully you can get more comfortable showing your very worst moments to your supervisor, because that's how you'll grow. But it's a scary process.

One of my best supervisors so far has been during my time in my master's program beginning my clinical work. He really made me think about what I did and what I said all within the space of the sessions I had with clients. I always trusted that he had my best interests in mind, and even in the face of struggling with a specific session, he would always find something positive I may not have noticed initially to further make me believe I am in the right profession.

—Jacqueline, second-year public MA student

Supervision is only partly about the client. The rest is about you and your reactions to your client. Do you like the client? Do you feel annoyed? Do you find the client attractive? Was your hesitation in session about your anxiety? How is this client like you? In some traditions, supervision will feel a lot like psychotherapy for you. In other traditions, it'll feel more educational. But in all cases, it's important to address reactions, responses, thoughts, and feelings about clients; these are vital pieces of data in the development of the therapeutic alliance and the effective delivery of treatment.

This focus on your reactions means that you'll need to be pretty open and vulnerable at times. This might end up being a different sort of relationship than you've ever had with a teacher. Although it's a working and professional relationship, there's a level of exposure and rawness that might be new to you. If your clinical supervisor is also your classroom instructor or research advisor, you'll have a complicated multiple relationship problem to navigate as well. Once you figure out what your supervisor wants from you (and you from them), my hope is that you can have a clear conversation with them about how you can best use the time you have with them.

My best supervisor modeled fantastic professional boundaries and a therapeutic demeanor that was pivotal for my growth.

—Chris, fourth-year private PsyD student

As is true with professors (see Chapter 2), your relationships with supervisors are important. Although they are hopefully motivated to help you grow as a clinician, supervisors also have evaluative power over you. And one thing to remember is that your clients aren't really *your* clients; they're the clinical purview of your supervisor. So, in *most cases*, you need to be sure to do what your supervisor instructs (because it's their license on the line). Be open to new ideas and allow them to stretch your limits; find what feels right to you and what doesn't. Be up front about where your growth edges are so that your supervisor can help you adapt to them appropriately.

I have been surprised about the great extent to which I rely on supervision.

—Fourth-year private PsyD student

In order to help trainees feel more prepared when they begin clinical work, I think it is important for supervisors to use self-disclosure regarding their own processes of professional development. This would both highlight the continual nature of developing as a clinician as well as normalize any feelings of unpreparedness that trainees are likely to experience. I also believe a nurturing environment in supervision, where individuals feel just as comfortable sharing successes as failures, comprises a fundamental component in helping trainees feel more prepared to begin clinical work.

—Ari, fourth-year public PhD student

Although it's rare, as a trainee, you might find yourself in an odd ethical situation from time to time in your supervisory relationship. In my career, I've heard of supervisors offering their supervisees drugs, suggesting that the student unnecessarily break confidentiality, telling the student to transfer wealthy patients to the supervisor's private practice, congratulating supervisees for getting assigned a "hot" client, never letting supervisees speak and just telling long and boring stories about their children, and making sexual advances toward students. Statistically speaking, none of these things are likely to happen to you, but if you ever feel uncomfortable about your supervisory relationship and/or you think your supervisor is acting unethically (or directing you to do so), you need to consult and take some action. When clients are involved, we have an even greater responsibility to keep our eyes open and follow our ethical mandates.

I had quite a negative experience with a past supervisor who was childish, condescending, demeaning, blaming, and close-minded. After wrongly accusing me of something I did not do and not allowing me to explain myself, this supervisor used (read: abused) his power, and I felt helpless.

—Fourth-year public PhD student

Occupational Hazards

In my third year of grad school, I worked in the child and adolescent units of an inpatient psychiatric hospital. I led groups and did individual and family therapy with a handful of kids on the units. In that year, I learned more about trauma, child abuse and maltreatment, family dysfunction, poverty, and racial, cultural, and sexual marginalization than I ever knew existed. The work was wonderful, inspiring, and a lot of fun, but it opened my eyes to a world of pain and suffering that I hadn't comprehended before. Luckily, I had a 90-minute drive home each day to help me decompress and process before I reentered the world of my friends, student colleagues, and loved ones. I think that I aged more in that one year than any other in my life.

This is a chapter on *starting* clinical work, so I won't talk about burnout or vicarious trauma here. You may find, however, that, depending on your own life story, the clinical stories you hear might rattle you more than you are expecting. And even if you've led a life marked by complexity, you might still grapple with how to contain the stories you hear. Even more than just the stimulus value of the stories themselves is the expectation that you, as a clinician, are supposed to be *helpful.* The feeling of inadequacy and helplessness that comes to *all* clinicians is one that we all need to address, particularly early in training. Indeed, a question that students often ask is "How do I keep from thinking about this all night?"

There's no easy answer to that question, but some degree of clinical compartmentalization comes in time. Even now, there are plenty of times that I'm rattled by a client or feel as though I could have handled a situation better. And those episodes stick in my mind, rob me of sleep, and disrupt my mood. It happens a lot less than it used to, but clinical challenges always remind me to be appreciative of my family and friends, to honor my role as a helper, and to acknowledge the limitations of my ability to rescue those who are suffering.

The First Year

Your first year of clinical training will be a megasteep learning curve. In your first few sessions, you'll have no clue what's going on or what you're supposed to say. With the aid of a compassionate, experienced, and supportive supervisor (and often peers), your work will be remarkably better by the end of the first year of practicum. You'll be amazed at how much you grow in that first year.

There are a number of things that new clinicians seem to be surprised to learn in that first year:

1. You'll be winging it more than you might expect. Even if you have the best supervisor in the world and you're following a strict manualized protocol, there will be a time in each session when you're flying a little blind. That's not a problem, but it's just the start of you flexing your clinical muscles. I'd argue that you're learning more in those moments when you feel completely off the rails and on your own than you do when things are more clear. Nothing teaches us more than being a little lost. The beauty of psychotherapy is that when you screw something up, you can generally come back to it in the next session and clean it up.

The most challenging thing about clinical work has been feeling like I have no idea what I am doing and feeling that way on a regular basis. People who get into psychology graduate programs have generally been high achievers who are more familiar with success than failure. So much of early clinical work revolves around uncertainty. Growing as a clinician doesn't just come from experience, but also from taking your worst moments and blinders to someone who is way better at this than you to have them watch it and work through how you could have handled it better, how to recover from a rupture, or problem solve next steps. It's a vulnerable process.

—Nicole, third-year private PsyD student

---

2. You won't like all of your clients. Sure, you'll have compassion for all of them and want to do right by them, but that doesn't mean you'll like them. I heard a supervisor once say that we always need to find something we don't like in each client because that helps us know what needs to change. As a supervisor, I always give students permission to dislike their clients (usually by voicing what it is that I dislike about their clients). Being aware of our feelings helps us not act on them, so airing our feelings about our clients (good and bad) will help us deliver the best care we can.

The number-one tip I would give to a new clinician is never underestimate the power of the therapeutic alliance. Fostering a sincere relationship where the client is truly seen is both one of the strongest mechanisms of therapeutic change and something that even beginning clinicians have the tools to accomplish.

—Ari, fourth-year public PhD student

The best part of clinical work so far is when I form a strong relationship with a client and feel like I am being a good therapist. Sometimes personalities just click, and that can really help the therapy move along.

—Fourth-year public PhD student

---

3. Change isn't neat the way it looks in textbooks. People are messy and complicated. Change isn't clean and linear, and progress comes at different rates for different folks. Don't be surprised when a really deep, intense, and moving session is followed by a really ho-hum one that risks boring you to tears. Growth isn't consistent, and clients often need a few recovery sessions to regroup. Learning how to ride those ups and downs of change will help you see the big picture of change and keep you from getting discouraged when things seem to be stalling out.

I was surprised that progress is not linear. Some days I felt like my work was so meaningful and my clients were bettering their lives, and some days I felt like I was not even sure if I believed in therapy as a treatment anymore. It is hard to accept that not everyone will improve or that not all improvements are quick and visible.

—Third-year private PsyD student

---

4. You'll need to be pretty self-directed and find your own helpful sources. Even the best supervisor can't teach you everything you need to know (and often supervisors don't know what you need to know), so you'll need

to buy some books, read some articles, and watch videos on your own. As is true for your research, you'll need to track down books, articles, and other materials to help flesh out your clinical knowledge. As a student, I read countless books and articles to help bolster my conceptual understanding of psychotherapy and the clients I was seeing; in fact, I probably read more on my own than I did for my classes. There's just too much to learn to leave it to class work or the direction of supervisors.

I was surprised and disappointed to learn that therapy is often learned from reading manuals and books. It is a lonelier process than I had imagined and independently learned to start. Certainly, there is art to doing therapy well. However, it didn't occur to me that that early clinical work was trying to closely follow a manual and work through work sheets.

—Third-year private PsyD student

I believe that more can be learned about the human experience through history's great authors than any psychology textbook. I would recommend that beginning clinicians expose themselves to as much of this type of reading as the demands of a training program will allow—it is also great for self-care. Personally, my clinical work is continually being informed by authors such as Aldous Huxley, D. H. Lawrence, and Leo Tolstoy.

—Ari, fourth-year public PhD student

---

5. **The work is an emotional roller coaster.** I think that, before I started seeing clients, I pictured psychotherapy as some dispassionate process that I provided *for* clients. It didn't take long for me to realize that psychotherapy is a process we engage in *with* clients. I felt their lows and their sadness, and I reveled in their happiness and successes. The joy and beauty of the work is the connection with others, but that connection often has a price tag of emotional exhaustion, particularly when you're new at it. I'll cover this subject more in the next chapter, but suffice it to say that unlike the work of classes, the emotional work of being a therapist is labor intensive on a different level.

Hands down, the best part of my clinical work thus far has been getting to learn from each of my clients.

—Fourth-year public PhD student

---

6. **Terminations can be really hard.** Terminations are part of psychotherapy, and you'll need to prepare yourself for the good-byes. Even if you don't

have a lot of terminations during the year, usually at the end of your first year of clinical work you'll need to wrap up and head to a new clinical placement. And that will bring a few endings. Terminations might be harder than you imagine, and they're often more difficult than clients imagine. Very few people have opportunities for *good good-byes*, but clinical terminations make that possible. You might have feelings of loss, relief, regret, pride, or sadness. Use terminations as a way to look back over the work you've done, acknowledge gains (in both yourself and your client), and reflect on what the client has meant to you. I often say that one of the most frustrating things about clinical work is that it's a series of stories where you can't find out the ending. We only share a brief moment in our patients' lives, and wrapping up those moments can bring out a lot of feelings for everyone. Be present to those feelings and allow the work to be meaningful.

I just had my termination session with a patient I saw transform into an entirely different person. It has been an incredible experience to watch him grow and get parts of his life back that he had thought were lost forever. Seeing people achieve their goals makes the hard moments worth it.

—Nicole, third-year private PsyD student

The reward of participating in my clients' personal growth has been the best part of clinical work thus far.

—Chris, fourth-year private PsyD student

Evidence-Based Practice and the Craft of Psychotherapy

My first supervisor and graduate school mentor, Dr. Mark Hilsenroth, referred to psychotherapy as a *craft*: a blend of science and art. This sentiment was well captured by the APA Presidential Task Force on Evidence-Based Practice (APA Presidential Task Force, 2006). Although evidence-based practice in psychology (EBPP) has somehow become a euphemism for some type of highly structured manualized treatment, the real definition is far more interesting. Simply put, as defined by APA, EBPP is the combination of research, clinical experience, and the needs, wishes, and background of the client. It is a *craft*.

As noted in the definition, part of the craft involves consulting research. I don't think anyone would argue that there's often a gulf between science and practice in psychology. But part of EBPP is making ample use of the science that is available to us to best serve the clients we treat. When I was a predoctoral intern, I went into my supervisor, Dr. Mark Blais's, office and asked him to help me interpret an MMPI-2 profile. After staring blankly at me for a few seconds, he asked, "And what did your comprehensive review of the literature tell you before you came in here to ask me that?" He was right. I hadn't done my homework and was trying to shortcut the literature review process (and I slunk back out of his office with my tail between my legs). Avail yourself of the science related to your theory, your clinical interventions, and the client populations you work with.

That said, psychotherapy is a craft, and research is only one part of the equation. Research is often limited, conflicting, and overly specific. It's likely that very few of your clients will cleanly fit the profiles of research participants, particularly with clients from underrepresented groups where intervention research is often lacking. Furthermore, it is unlikely that you'll be able to deliver a treatment protocol with the same fidelity as clinicians in a research study (not that you'd want to). And blindly following a treatment manual runs the risk of being inflexible with the needs of your clients and making you feel like a mere technician and not a clinician.

I say all of this to emphasize that you should make consultation of research a habit that you develop in the early days of your clinical training. Although the data aren't often clean or entirely enlightening, there is much to learn from research. In addition, when you find significant gaps in the literature, you've also found potential dissertation topics, which helps to bridge the science-to-practice and practice-to-science divides.

· · · · · · · · · · · · · · · · · **Tips and Strategies** · · · · · · · · · · · · · · · · · ·

1. Focus on the relationship and be curious about their experience.
2. Expect to feel vulnerable as a clinician and a supervisee.
3. Visit the literature on both theory and technique.
4. Be prepared for supervision and think about what you'd like to accomplish during supervision meetings.

· ·

Your first few steps as a clinician won't be your best. The process is long and will involve a lot of mistakes and a lingering sense of inadequacy. But it's a gift to be able to do this work, and I urge you to approach it with joy and humility. Everyone starts somewhere, and you, too, will get better at it. No matter what, after your first session, you'll be a therapist. Welcome to the profession.

Reference

APA Presidential Task Force on Evidence-Based Practice. (2006). Evidence-based practice in psychology. *American Psychologist*, *61*, 271–285.

CHAPTER 6

How to Be You . . . as a Therapist

In my first few months of doing psychotherapy, I was doing little more than impersonating a therapist. I'd never been in therapy myself at that point, so, from watching videos, reading books, and listening to my supervisor, I had some vague idea of what being a therapist looked like—a very vague idea, in fact. I sat nice and straight, I leaned in when the client was talking about *important things*, and when I didn't know what else to say (which was often), I'd say, "Say more about that," or "That's important." I'm not sure I was actually doing therapy as much as just pretending to be a therapist.

It took a while before the words that were coming out of my mouth felt like my words, the way I was interacting with my clients felt genuine, and I was really bringing myself to the clinical situation. Having watched a number of student clinicians over the years, this is always part of the journey (or it should be): changing from *pretending* to be a therapist to actually *being yourself* as a therapist.

Certainly, the pretending part is an important step. When we're new at something, it makes sense to pretend or to copy someone with more knowledge or experience. Indeed, when I started teaching, I was merely doing my best impression of Dr. Larry White, one of my favorite undergraduate professors. Pretending is important in learning any process.

I can't speak for all supervisors on this, and maybe even some would disagree with me, but one of the most important things for any clinician to learn is to be comfortable being themselves in the therapy room. No therapist should ever deliver the exact same treatment as another because the person of the therapist is an important part of the treatment. The differences between you and other therapists will allow you to say things that they can't and to see things they won't. My job as a supervisor is to help students find *their* voice and *their* style, and not just be another version of me (one is enough!). Once you get the hang of the basics, trying to fit yourself into a cookie-cutter notion of what a *therapist* is is a real disservice to the field.

That said, the version of you that is a therapist might be somewhat different from the you that your friends and family know. Professionalism is good, but, if taken too far, you run the risk of being a distant caricature. Part of learning to be yourself as a therapist is knowing which parts of you you need to *tone down* and which parts you need to *amplify*. Although you can fine-tune your personal presentation, you shouldn't try to be someone you're not. For me, working with kids taught me very quickly that I needed to be genuine, honest, and "real." An adolescent can smell phony nonsense from a mile away (and will most certainly say something about it).

If a supervisor tells you that you need to tone down or adjust parts of yourself, take that information and reflect on it. It's likely that you'll feel some sense of embarrassment, anger, or shame about having to change some of your interpersonal behaviors or dress, particularly those that you've not been aware of before or that you feel are defining personal characteristics or cultural markers. In due time, you'll have the freedom to choose how you want to be as a therapist, but, as a student, you don't have much leeway on that yet. Take the feedback and try to adapt and see how that feels.

In my early training, I received feedback that I could be a bit *too* informal. As you can probably tell by reading this book, I tend to lean toward informality and some degree of straightforwardness. I had supervisors who told me that I needed to tighten up and be more formal, but others gave me more leeway to be my folksy self. Given those conflicting messages, it was hard at times to find a style that felt professional enough to honor the importance of the work and informal enough that it still felt like me. That balance is probably still in flux as I continue to gain experience and comfort with myself and my role as a therapist.

All of this hopefully serves to illustrate that the process of becoming yourself as a therapist will be (or at least should be) an ongoing goal. Of course, *yourself* is also always in flux, so this whole exchange might end up being like shooting at a moving target. And the style you have now won't be the style you'll have in 10 years (hopefully) because you'll be older and have more experience (both clinical experience and life experience). Certainly, there are things that I can say to clients now that I never could have said to them 15 years ago, simply because I'm older. No matter what style you gravitate toward, make sure that it feels good and consistent with at least one part of who you are, and remember that it will change.

· · · · · · · · · · · · · · · · ·   **Words of Wisdom**   · · · · · · · · · · · · · · · · ·

1. The process of becoming a therapist is becoming yourself as a therapist. This process starts in graduate school but will take years.
2. Don't stress too much about having a theoretical orientation. Be open to ideas and read literature on both theory and technique.
3. We all have limits of personal competency that are different from professional competency. Know what your limits are.
4. Be vocal about your change with family and loved ones.

The Tribalism of Theoretical Orientation

It won't be long into your graduate career before you'll need to identify which theoretical orientation camp you belong to. Often you'll need to defend or explain your orientation during your qualifying exams, and there's even an essay question about orientation on the application you'll fill out for internships. In my mind, asking students about their theoretical orientation is like asking someone to get married to someone they've only just met. How can you possibly know?

I would guide any new clinician to worry less about his or her "theoretical orientation" and focus instead on honing the common vital elements of most any form of psychotherapy.

—Chris, fourth-year private PsyD student

There are some limited data on orientation choice as a function of students' personality dispositions (see Arthur, 2001, for a review), which suggests that the choice of a conceptual model is not entirely a data-based decision. Moreover, more and more psychologists are identifying as *integrated* in orientation, choosing to systematically combine different parts of different theories. Indeed, to paraphrase many of the students I've supervised, "They kind of all sound the same to me, and they're just using different words to say the same things." I'll argue that there's more to it than that, but maybe not a whole lot more.

I am so intrigued by all the different styles and orientations out there. They all seem pretty cool to me, and I don't want to "settle down" and miss out on all the other good stuff that certain styles offer. That's nice and dandy when thinking about it abstractly, but people ask you these questions, and it's good to have a clearer understanding of the way you do therapy: for you, for your clients, and for the people interviewing you for a job or internship someday. I am still searching, but I am reading a lot to find out what sits right with me. I think that's what it comes down to. What sits right? What makes sense to you? Because you have to believe in it if you are going to use it successfully. I have come to terms with the fact that I am still in the process of discovering this, and I've had to do a lot of acceptance of that for now. I am hoping that it will start to take shape with more reading, watching, and doing.

—Fourth-year public PhD student

So, how to make sense of any of it? My guess is that we find an orientation the way we gravitate toward a lot of things: someone we like or admire teaches us about it, or it makes sense given our personal experience. No matter what, I'd urge you to not cling too tightly to a theoretical orientation because it's bound to change and grow (hopefully). In any case, research seems pretty clear that none of them are superior to the others, so even if you choose at random, you won't be wrong. In my opinion, it seems that the only folks who have a quick and easy answer to "What's your theoretical orientation?" are people who don't do much clinical work. People are complex, and experience makes things more complicated, not less. So, if you're stressing about joining camp CBT, ACT, or object relations (or any of the other myriad ways of understanding the human condition), don't. Just choose something that makes sense to you now and have the cognitive flexibility to adapt and change as needed. Now probably isn't the time for dogmatism.

> The most stressful part about learning clinical practice, for me, has been figuring out my theoretical orientation. It has been quite a journey that I am still on, and I have plenty of reading and exploring to go before I feel comfortable and confident saying how change works and what therapy truly is.
>
> —Josh, fourth-year public PhD student

I think it's useful here to differentiate between a clinical *theory* and a clinical *technique*. A theory should be a way of understanding the whole of humanity, including yourself, your friends, your third-grade teacher, your mom, scary clowns, your clients, and everyone else. A theory should include both normal and abnormal behavior and a broad idea of what makes us human. As I often say, "There's no *just* in psychology," meaning that, as a psychologist, you can't say that a person *just* wanted to, *just* decided, *just* did it, *just* is that way. As a psychologist, you need to have a way of understanding and explaining all of human behavior; there is no *just*—there's always a reason.

As opposed to a clinical theory, a clinical technique is what happens in the therapy room to help bring about change for a particular client. For example, although I have a broad psychodynamic orientation (meaning that I understand all of humanity through a generally psychodynamic lens), what I do in the therapy room borrows heavily from ACT and CBT. Granted, I understand those techniques from a psychodynamic perspective, but I'm happy to use the tools that are derived from other orientations. So, all of this illustrates that the "What's your orientation?" question is seemingly pretty complicated—so complicated, in fact, that it's almost not worth stressing about. Read, watch, think, reflect, and listen and you'll find your way toward something that fits well with you. And as one of my supervisors used to say, "Orientation should be like slippers worn soft," meaning that no matter what, your humanity and the alliance should be in the foreground.

> I have found that committing to a style of psychotherapy that is not in alignment with my supervisor or institution is apt to fail. In many ways, to adapt is to succeed.
>
> —Chris, fourth-year private PsyD student

Utility and Futility

In my fourth year of graduate school, I was called and told that one of my clients had attempted suicide by taking an overdose of sleeping pills in his truck in the parking lot of a local grocery store. In the 12 hours before I got the call, he'd been taken to the hospital, medically stabilized, and discharged. This was a client whom I'd been seeing for two years and with whom I had a great relationship. As is often true for suicide attempts, his was relatively impulsive and not the result of a prolonged or acute depression. As might be expected, I freaked. I was frightened, guilty, and angry (he didn't even *try* to contact me beforehand!). Mostly I felt futile and useless. After two years of (what I thought to be) really good therapy, my client had tried to kill himself. It was a horrible experience.

Flash forward to just a couple of years ago: I received an email from a young woman whom I had seen for three years when she was a teenager, some ten years prior. "You were the only person I felt comfortable enough with to open up with, be myself, and know I wasn't being looked at like a juvenile delinquent," it read. "You helped me to see that there was more to me than I was told and I learned to be accountable for my life and stop digging myself deeper into a hole." This client had gone on to foster a solid circle of family, friends, and the start of a rewarding career. It's hard to explain how much that note meant to me; it was an indication that, at least for this one client, I had been helpful.

These two stories illustrate that clinical work is often a ride of utility and futility. Sometimes this is related to a particular client, a type of client, a type of clinical relationship, or a particular time in our lives as therapists. No matter what, we all need to make some peace with the truth that we can't always be helpful, or as helpful as we wish we could be. I've often said to clients something like "I wish I could do or say something to magically ease your suffering, but I just can't do that." Often that's enough to help the patient feel seen and understood, but it's hard to acknowledge our own futility. For me, I've made some peace with the idea that change is the purview of the client and I'm merely a helper. That is, I lack the control to truly bring about change in another human being; only they can do that. Research tells us that *most* therapy patients get better or have some notable improvement, but when facing those clients and cases where change is slow, incremental, or nonexistent, it's hard to sit with the sense of futility.

I have realized that I am not powerful enough to "fix" everything that my clients bring in. It is really hard to bear witness to aspects of life that you cannot influence. At the same time, it is a source of relief to remind myself that I am not powerful enough to "fix" everything. It is this balance that I find challenging.

—Natalie, third-year private PsyD student

I think that supervision and consultation is a great start to managing clinical stress; to let the weight of some of your cases be held by others for a bit can really take some of the personal stress off. In addition, I remind myself that sometimes clinical work will be stressful, while other times it will be relaxing or validating, and if I can learn to roll with the waves of clinical work, then I will fare better.

—Josh, fourth-year public PhD student

As a new therapist, you will likely grapple with feelings of futility as well. And that sense of futility might dovetail with your sense of insecurity about your experience and abilities as a therapist. "Maybe I'm not cut out for this!" "Maybe I should be an administrator or researcher instead." "Maybe I should get a job in a bakery or something. I love cake!" It's true that you might not be as helpful to people in the beginning of your training as you will be eventually, but when things feel futile, check in with a supervisor, take good care of yourself, and do what you can to be helpful. No matter what, sometimes the best we have is a *desire* to be helpful.

The most stressful element I have encountered in learning clinical practice has been overcoming the initial desire to have all the answers or know the perfect intervention for a given client need.

— Ari, fourth-year public PhD student

The moments of utility as a therapist are wonderful and make the futile moments worthwhile. Most of us find our way to this field because (a) we're trying to figure out ourselves and/or our wacko families, and (b) we want to be helpful. Those times when we have a good relationship with a client, get a note of thanks, or really see important change can sustain us during the darker moments when we really are limited. The beauty of the work is the dance between futility and utility, and learning how to tolerate that dance is an important part of graduate training (and beyond).

I really love creating safe, healing, and meaningful spaces for my clients. I love actually verbalizing that this is their space and that we can shape it to be whatever they need it to be. I love being let into someone's life and learning about their worldview.

— Natalie, third-year private PsyD student

Boundaries, Competency, and Limits

Part of becoming a psychologist is learning what your limits are. For bright and motivated students, you might not be comfortable with the idea that you *have* limits, but limits are important for helping to keep us sane. We have limits of time, energy, intellectual capacity, emotional reserve, and professional competence. Although we might have the desire to be superhuman, it's rare that any of us are.

Part of knowing our limits is knowing which clients we like, which we don't, which we can't tolerate, which we like too much, and which activate us too much to even work with. When asked, most students will say that they couldn't work with sex offenders, folks with difficult interpersonal tendencies (e.g., personality disorders), kids with developmental disorders, or folks who have hurt children. Certainly these populations can all be challenging, but you should also think carefully about the types of clients or issues that you might find activating on a more subtle or personal level. How do you feel about men, women, ethnic minorities, overweight people, uneducated people, liberals or conservatives, wealthy or poor people, left handers, or the blue eyed? A little facetious, yes, but part of our competence means that we need to examine subtle biases that lie in the gray area that precedes a true boundary. Some of that will be social stigma, as well as personal stigmas based on where we're from or what we've experienced.

For example, I don't work with people in my practice who have primary issues with substance abuse. I'm not clinically competent to do so because I lack the extensive training needed to work with that population. But the reason that I don't have that training is because, given my extensive family history of substance abuse, I chose, as a student, to steer clear of those issues. At the time of my training, they were too close to home, and my own emotional baggage back then might have gotten in the way of doing effective work with that population.

Some boundaries and edges will reveal themselves to you now, but others will emerge over time. You should always be on the lookout to stretch those boundaries and push yourself in places that you might feel uncomfortable. But it's important that you know yourself well enough to be on the lookout for emotional danger zones that might have negative consequences for your clients. Again, it's an ongoing process, and a good supervisor can be really helpful in sorting it all out.

Related to limits are your own personal boundaries with time and energy. Plenty has been written about clinical boundaries and self-disclosure, and I won't discuss those here. But part of setting boundaries in clinical work means that you'll disappoint people who count on you or who are in crisis. For example, I was supervising a student a few years ago who was scheduled up to her eyeballs. She was preparing for her qualifying exams, getting a paper ready for a conference, and writing papers for finals. And, of course, one of her clients called to ask for an additional session. In our supervision meeting, the student noted that she could see her client if she canceled the date she had planned for that evening. "How would you feel about canceling your date to see your client?" I asked. "Pretty resentful and angry, I guess. It's the only non-school thing I'm doing this week, and he's not in that big of a crisis," she said. "And how would you feel if you went on the date and made your client wait a few days until finals are over?" She said, "Guilty, and like I was letting my client down." "So which do you think is better for your client: seeing him while feeling resentful or taking care of yourself while feeling some guilt?" "I think I'll go on my date and deal with it," she said. It was a good call. As psychologists, we're always so good at *sacrificing* ourselves and our time for someone else, but I'd urge you to be a little selfish from time to time in the interest of maintaining your sanity and endurance over the long haul.

Boundaries can be hard because sometimes you want to spend five more minutes with a client to hammer home a point, or perhaps they are crying and you feel bad cutting them off. Perhaps also, they are doorknob clients who like to bring up something important or serious toward the end of the session. Usually I am flexible if time permits for those who need a minute to gather themselves or if I feel like two more minutes would benefit the client. Otherwise, I usually say that the new topic sounds interesting and that we should pick it up at the beginning of the next session. I have been fortunate enough so far to not have to deal with many other kinds of boundary issues yet.

—Fourth-year public PhD student

Heart Fatigue

Like I mentioned in Chapter 5, psychotherapy is a process we engage in *with* our clients. As is true for all of us, their lives have ups and downs, victories and setbacks. The gift of being a therapist is that we get to be there with them during these times of success and failure. Psychoanalytic theorist Heinz Kohut posited that the active ingredient of psychotherapy is empathy. Carl Rogers emphasized empathy and attunement as well. When your heart is attuned to what the client is feeling, effective and therapeutic words will follow. It's in those moments of attunement that you'll begin to be able to see their world from their perspective. Your heart needs to go where their heart is, because that's the path toward empathy and helping. If your client is sad, you'll need to connect with your own sense of sadness. If they are anxious, you'll need to connect with your experience of anxiety. If they're happy, you can be happy with them. And if they've just won the lottery, you can empathetically raise your fee. When I used to do a lot of grief work with kids who had lost their parents, parents who had lost children, and others who were dealing with loss, I was moved to tears along with my clients on a handful of occasions. It was heart work.

For an hour, this type of heart exercise is fine, but consider what happens at the end of a full clinical day. It's not uncommon for a graduate student to see five or six clients in a given day or to have a handful of clients and engage in some consultation work with a teacher or workplace. It's a lot. And the ups and downs of the heart work can be really exhausting. Like any other muscle, your heart can get tired and worn out.

For me, and for many other therapists I know, a full day of heart work can lead to some degree of emotional numbing at the end of the day. You might find that you really want to check out, that you're increasingly distracted when trying to do class work, or that it's challenging to be fully present with your loved ones. All of that is normal. As with many other aspects of life, the important thing is what you do about it. My advice is to pay attention to how you're feeling and recognize when you lack the capacity to be connected with others (or when you really need to be with others) or when your heart is too tired to deal with your statistics homework. If you don't make it a habit, you can take a night off. And if you can't take a night off, at least give yourself some decompression time before you need to dive into your regression equation homework. It's also good to be on top of your calendar so you can reasonably predict when you'll be too fried to get much other work done or have a first date. Knowing and planning for a lack of capacity is always a good idea, even if you surprise yourself with how much energy you have left over.

Rewriting Your Story

Related to the issue of heart work is self-work. I've alluded to this topic in other chapters, but graduate school in general, and learning to be a therapist in particular, will force you into some serious self-reflection. Some of you are good at that already. (In fact, some of you are probably *too* good at that already.) No matter your experience or predilection toward self-reflection, you might be confronted with more than you've had to deal with before.

Just like your clients, you have a story about your life. And just like your clients, the story you tell yourself is probably not entirely true. Images you have of relationships with family and friends, experiences of pain and discomfort you had, and even the reasons that you came into the field in general might be cast in a new light. The process of supervision, the classes you take, and the emotional experiences you have while sitting with clients will force you to take a different look at yourself and your life story. And you might not always like what you find there. Indeed, a number of students have come to me after a year or so of graduate school with a statement like "I thought that my family was pretty normal, but now I see how [caustic/damaging/weird/inappropriate/distant/enmeshed] things were," or "I see the relationship I had with [relationship partner] as being a lot different than it really was." It's heavy stuff, but it's a necessary process and you're not alone in going through it.

I'm making this all sound really dark, and that's often not the case at all. I've found that many graduate students discover a greater sense of peace, honesty, and compassion during their time in graduate school. As they reevaluate themselves and their lives, they come to a more genuine understanding of themselves, who they are, and why they've needed to be such overachieving do-gooders (for example). I wish for all of you what I wish for my patients: that the painful work of change leads to greater freedom and a deeper sense of authenticity.

Of course, the thing to watch for is a shift in the relationships you have with others. Graduate school will change you, even if it's merely a function of age and spending too much time with statistics professors. I often warn psychotherapy clients that when they change, their relationships might shift in a way that makes things complicated. Like all organisms, we like homeostasis, so when we're involved in a relationship with someone who is changing or going through something challenging (even if it's for the best), we can find it dysregulating or even off putting. What this means for you is that, as you are changed through the process of graduate school, you might feel more strain in your relationships than you've felt before.

For example, I entered graduate school as a relatively sensitive and empathetic guy, but not particularly brimming with insight. There were aspects of my life, my family, and my childhood that I was motivated to keep unexamined. Working with clients who were suffering forced me to examine my own experiences of loss, leading to lots of painful self-reflection. I realized that some of my clients were capable of greater self-reflection than I was, leading me to examine the barriers I had erected. At the same time, I was in a relationship that had begun years earlier during my undergraduate years. As I changed and allowed myself more insight about how I was and what I wanted, the relationship couldn't expand to accommodate the newer version of me. From there, things went from bad to worse.

Now, I'm not writing this to freak you out about your relationships with your family and loved ones (well . . . maybe a little bit) but merely to alert you to a process that might happen in your journey to becoming a psychologist. The best way to deal with change is to anticipate it before it happens, so be thoughtful and perhaps even vocal with your loved ones about what it is you're going through. Don't hesitate to seek out therapy for yourself (see Chapter 11) for a little support along the way.

Change is hard. It's hard for our clients, and it's hard for us. Hopefully, though, the change is worth it in that we find ourselves more at peace, with greater empathy, and with more attunement to our needs and those of others.

Finding Your Clinical Superpower

You have a superpower. You might not know it yet, but you do. For many of you, your superpower is buried deep inside, and you don't think of it as a superpower. My guess is that you think of it as a weakness or a problem. And that might be true, but it's also a superpower. I'll explain.

Years ago, when I was interviewing for my internship at Mass General, Dr. Steve Durant asked me this question: "All psychologists need a way to understand two things: human diversity and what it means to suffer. Tell me about how you understand diversity and how you understand suffering." What he was *really* asking me about in that question was my own experience of feeling like an outsider, of feeling lost, overlooked, and in pain. He wanted to know that I knew what it was like to suffer, because without some knowledge of suffering, how can we be with others who are in pain?

All of you have suffered. No matter where you come from and what type of life you've had, you have suffered. Sure, maybe you haven't suffered in a really dramatic way, but all suffering is suffering, no matter how it might appear to others. Suffering isn't fun, but it's the thing that allows us to connect with clients and to stand strong when they need us to be there. Our experience of anxiety, depression, fear of clowns, feeling not quite good enough, feeling insecure, feeling too nerdy, too dumb, too smart, too silly, too serious, too short, too tall, too fat, too thin, too damaged, too good, too rich, too poor, and just too much—those are the sources of our empathy and connection. Harnessing those insecurities and allowing yourself to be present to them will give you so much more insight into the lives of your clients and help you find the words that they need to hear. This is your clinical superpower. Use it wisely.

1. Accept feedback from your supervisor with an open mind.
2. Stretch to experiment with different techniques and ways of being a therapist.
3. Make some peace with futility.
4. Be ready and prepared for some degree of heart fatigue. Take care of yourself before you feel the need to do so.

· ·

The role of being a therapist is a gift and a challenge. We are given the opportunity and responsibility for sitting with others during some of their darkest moments. We share in the joy of their triumphs and the sadness of their losses. And the thing we have to offer is ourselves, our knowledge, and the craft of our discipline. As you navigate the waters of your training, remember that what got you to graduate school was a hearty mix of perseverance, intellect, and interpersonal skill. The job of a therapist requires all of those things. Never lose sight of what got you to the place you are; those tools and that experience (good and bad) will make you the therapist you will become.

Reference

Arthur, A. R. (2001). Personality, epistemology, and psychotherapists' choice of theoretical model: A review and analysis. *European Journal of Psychotherapy, Counseling, and Health, 4,* 45–64.

CHAPTER 7

Milestones and Rites of Passage

In May of my fourth year of graduate school, I stood alone in an empty classroom and slowly packed up my computer and my notes. Moments before, my committee had paraded past offering handshakes after I had successfully defended my dissertation (with no revisions!). And just like that, after a year and a half of writing, collecting data, endless statistics, revisions, and preparation, I was done with the academic portion of my graduate work. All that remained was my internship.

It was an odd moment. There were no fireworks, no balloons, and no magical transformation. Because I hadn't started internship yet, there was still another year before I became a "doctor," so I didn't even get the satisfaction of ordering new business cards. It was just me, my computer, and an empty classroom.

So many of the biggest moments in graduate school are like this: kind of anticlimactic. Milestones are not often well recognized or well celebrated by graduate programs, which can make it seem like they're not very important. The danger of that perspective is that it can make you jaded and left feeling like defending your dissertation, passing qualifying exams, starting practica, and so on are "no big deal." Just because they're not well recognized doesn't make them no big deal! They are, in fact, very big deals, but it's your job to recognize them and celebrate them (in a way that feels ego syntonic to you) even if no one celebrates with you.

One of the exciting, and exhausting, things about graduate school is that every year involves milestones. First time stepping onto an inpatient unit; first time presenting in case conference; first paper; dissertation; internship. The most relieving milestone was probably dissertation, because that felt the most daunting.

—Seth, predoctoral intern, private PhD student

The work never stops! If you're someone who is future oriented or has a tendency toward perfectionism (come on, I know it's not just me), it is all too easy to ruminate over your past missteps or feel like you're constantly moving toward an elusive goal. If you don't slow down and recognize your own milestones (and change your definition of success while you're at it), you're setting yourself up for failure.

— Audrey, fourth-year private PsyD student

My greatest achievement in graduate school is that now I can live more honestly with myself, and by extension with the people around me, and with more vitality in the world.

— Fourth-year public PhD student

If I were to compile a list of milestones of graduate school, it would look like this (in no particular order):

Finishing first quarter/semester	Finishing first year
Starting first practica	Publishing first paper
Presenting at first conference	Passing qualifying exams
Completing last class	Advancing to candidacy
Proposing thesis	Defending thesis
Completing first practica	Starting personal therapy
Proposing dissertation	Completing statistics courses
Making a good friend in the program	Applying for internship
First internship interview	Matching at internship site
Graduation	Starting internship
Taking on a leadership position	Having a failure experience

The list could go on and on depending on your program, your personality, and your background. But you can see in the list I have here that many of these experiences will go largely unrecognized. Your faculty advisor might not be too excited for your first paper publication, but it's important that you are. Your family might not get the big deal about the leadership position you've assumed, but it's important that you are. You might be too relieved at finishing statistics or other course work to recognize that it's a transition point, but take a moment and give yourself some credit. It's important. It will keep you going when you're having those down moments.

My biggest milestone during graduate school has been starting a family. I could not have anticipated the turns my personal life would take as I embarked on my professional training, but getting married and having a baby while in school has been incredibly challenging and rewarding. On the easy days, there's no one I would rather share my successes with than my wife, and on the difficult days, coming home to my delightful daughter and seeing her learn and play helps to ease some of the heaviness that this work carries.

—Audrey, fourth-year private PsyD student

Our training director often sends emails encouraging us to take the time to appreciate what we have accomplished. I really liked feeling supported by her in that way.

—Fourth-year private PsyD student

Nearly 25 years ago, I left the psychology building after the last class period of the last course I took in graduate school. It was an evening class, so it was dark outside. As I walked across campus toward my apartment, I stopped in front of the Old Main building on campus that was lit up and picturesque in the soft lighting. I took just a minute to think back on the years of work, challenge, success, and failure. I took a minute to think, *I'm done with all my classes*. It was a moment that could've been lost in thoughts about moving to start internship, work I still needed to do on my dissertation, or challenges in practicum, but I forced myself to have a mindful moment. And 25 years later, I still recall it in some detail. Find those moments in your life and make the experience as rich as possible.

Take time to celebrate and acknowledge significant milestones in a way that feels good for you. There is no right way to acknowledge your achievements, but acknowledging them can give you some good feelings that will sustain you until you make it to your next milestone.

—Lauren, predoctoral intern, public PhD student

Take time to celebrate your successes, no matter how small they may seem!

—Audrey, fourth-year private PsyD student

Celebrate the little things! Graduate school is a marathon, and there will be countless long days and challenging times. So when you accomplish something—even if it's small—share that with people and let yourself feel really good about it!

> You don't need to wait until you earn your degree, or a big milestone along the way such as passing qualifying exams, to celebrate your growth.
>
> —Josh, fourth-year public PhD student

> Giving advice to a new graduate student about grad school in general feels a little bit futile, since it seems to be one of those processes in which virtually all of the important lessons are both highly individual and painfully experiential. But with reference to milestones in particular, I would caution against pinning one's sense of accomplishment and professional identity on checking off those departmentally contrived boxes. Instead, I would encourage students to recognize that grad school is a constant process of being ground down and built back up, and that it is important and perhaps even necessary to appreciate the less tangible but ultimately more definitive milestones, such as the first client session in which you feel that you really helped someone . . . or the first time you can leave an incredibly demoralizing session with a sense of determination and purpose instead of self-recrimination. Or maybe even just finishing your stats homework without crying or having a drink partway through.
>
> —Evelyn, fourth-year public PhD student

The Three Big Barriers: Thesis, Qualifying Exams, and Dissertation

Although you might feel at times that the barriers in grad school are nearly endless, I like to think of the thesis, qualifying exams, and dissertation as the three big barriers of doctoral graduate studies (to be fair, "academic red tape" could be a fourth barrier). Not all doctoral programs will have all three of these requirements (and some have more), but these are pretty typical. These three barrier steps mean different things about your phase of training and your movement toward independence. Let's take a quick look at each one.

> Sometimes it feels like I'm on a hamster wheel; there's always something else to work toward in graduate school.
>
> —Fourth-year private PsyD student

Thesis

If you're in a terminal master's degree program, the thesis is your crowning academic achievement. In fact, in many terminal MA/MS programs, the thesis is a stronger product than it is in many doctoral programs where it's merely another requirement along the journey. But given that this section is about the three obstacles of doctoral studies, let's focus our attention there.

If you are in a doctoral program that requires an MA/MS thesis as part of your studies, it's best to think of it as a dissertation dress rehearsal. It's expected that the thesis be of high quality, but probably less in size and scope than the dissertation project. It's a place for you to consolidate research skills and demonstrate proficiency with study design, statistics, and data collection. It's also a time for you to find out (if you haven't already) that research always takes longer than you think it will; I always tell students that Actual Project Completion Time = 1.5 × Anticipated Project Completion Time. Depending on the quality of your undergraduate preparation, your thesis might be a bit redundant in size and scope to an honors thesis you might have completed.

Some programs might suggest that your thesis should be a publishable document, and some are more focused on the quality of the literature review. No matter what, be clear about what the requirements are. As is true for all phases of graduate school, it's good to get comfortable with asking mentors and advisors what they expect of you and your performance.

Given that the thesis is often the smaller cousin of the dissertation, it's tempting to dismiss it or not try to produce a quality product. Especially for those of you headed toward careers in academia or academically oriented hospitals, consider the thesis an opportunity to produce a publishable research paper. Your professors might expect this of you anyway, but even if they don't, ask whether your project might be publication worthy or appropriate for presentation at a conference. And even if you're headed toward a career in practice, consider the thesis a great opportunity to learn some skills that will make your dissertation less painful and onerous; your future self will thank you for it.

Qualifying Exams, Comprehensive Exams, Candidate Exams, Etc.

Nearly all programs have some sort of qualifying exam that students need to pass before advancing to doctoral candidacy. There are nearly as many variants of this as there are programs. In my experience, some programs have one big annual exam, some require topical papers, some require portfolios of work, and some even allow students to take the professional licensure exam (i.e., EPPP). My university also requires an oral defense in addition to exam materials.

No matter the format, qualifying exams tend to require an intense period of studying and/or writing, usually in addition to completing required course work. The exams typically cover ethics, basic psychological knowledge (e.g., biological and social psychology), clinical interventions and/or theory, research methodology, and some specialized knowledge area that's unique to the student. In some programs, a fail at the level of the qualifying exam means that you're kindly shown the exit from the program.

Finishing my qualifying exams was the most weirdly exhilarating milestone to reach: I was literally in shock. I just sat at the table with my advisor while the rest of my committee went to sign the paperwork and I kept asking if it was really happening, as though maybe they were playing an elaborate, incredibly mean joke on me. There is something that is simultaneously overwhelming yet anticli-mactic about having years of fear and anxiety culminate in an understated "OK, you're good to go, sign here." But I really did feel like a different person walking out of the room than I did walking in.

—Evelyn, fourth-year public PhD student

So, for those of you who are grappling with quals-related angst at the moment, allow me to let you in on a little secret: I failed my exam. Mind you, I didn't fail catastrophically, but I totally bungled Tarasoff in a way that was crystal clear to me as soon as it was pointed out. But it was too late. My program allowed me to write a couple of papers to demonstrate that I understood *duty to warn/protect*, and I was good to go. Even though it ended up being a mess that I could clean up, I was still pretty devastated and angry that I had made such a mistake after several months of studying. I lived. I got my PhD. I became a professor. Flowers still bloom, and my family still loves me.

All of this leads me to quals-related stress syndrome (QRSS). Apart from the internship application process (covered in a later chapter), I've found QRSS to be one of the greatest sources of graduate student angst. My guess is that there are two primary psychological issues for students to wrestle with during the qualifying exam process: uncertain expectations and good performer tendencies. No matter what, because the exam is an exam (or something similar), your faculty can only give you so much guidance and direction. You should have a clear sense of the test format, general content, and pragmatics (time limits, structure, etc.), but there will be a lot of unknowns (e.g., specific questions to be asked, expectations for performance, clinical curveballs, and perhaps even rogue graders). Some qualifying exams cover *all of psychology*; how can that not be anxiety provoking? Where do you even start? The unknowns lead to stress.

The other stressor for most graduate students is that you are pretty used to doing very, very well on exams. If you weren't hot at exams, you wouldn't be in grad school. You're used to performing well, and your exams have probably been a source of pride (or at least comfort) for you in the past. Your exam-taking muscle is well developed. So when you're poised to take a Very Important Exam, you get anxious, it ignites some old test-taking anxiety, and you feel the need to prove yourself or perform in the way that you're used to. In most programs, you can't really fail (although you might need to retake it), and exams are based on a pass/no pass threshold, but anxiety persists nonetheless.

Milestones are important, and as you approach them they often feel scarier than they are. You have been learning all along, during grad school, prior to grad school, and outside of school altogether. Pursuing your milestones are moments in your program where you can pause, synthesize all of this learning, and have really neat conversations with faculty who help you see the depths and limits of your knowledge. Just breathe through it, open your eyes, and enjoy the learning experience of going through the milestones.

—Fourth-year public PhD student

My advice about qualifying exams is to try to keep some perspective. When I talk to students after their exams, they feel relief, but also pride—not just pride at having passed the exam but also that they feel like experts in a field they've been working in for years. Hopefully, at the time of your qualifying exam, you will know more about psychology than you ever have before. If you recognize that fact, it can be a pretty important moment. So, yes, it's an exam and a quasi-hazing ritual, but if you can personalize it as an opportunity to coalesce your learning into a demonstrable moment, you might enjoy the moment more (or hate the moment less). No matter what, remember that there's probably a big safety net in your program, and not passing the exam the first time just means that you have more hassle to deal with, not that you're a failure as a human being who shouldn't be in graduate school.

Comps was better the more I made it about what I wanted to study and get to know better. However, passing does give you more power and voice because you've undergone the crucible and you join the club of the academy (I think, but maybe it's not true in reality).

—Fourth-year public PhD student

Quals was a ton of writing, synthesizing information, revising, and cramming. When I first approached this milestone, I was very intimidated by the oral component. As the time drew nearer and nearer, I realized that there was only so much I could cram in my brain. I had to take the approach that I would not be going into orals if I did not think my faculty advisor thought I was ready for them. It was a time to enjoy the learning experience, demonstrate my understanding of concepts I had learned, and show the limits to my knowledge.

—Fourth-year public PhD student

Milestones may look and feel insignificant, but celebrating them is very important! The finish line is a long ways away, so it is important to cheer when you finish each lap.

—Fourth-year public PhD student

I passed qualifying exams; yet the process felt confusing and archaic. It was frustrating to hear about other programs that had a comps process that seemed to be more intentionally designed to help students further their academic career, not just prove how much or little they know. Some programs have you write a literature review that you can later publish, or design a research project. These projects have a real and applied component that I find useful and motivating, and at the same time they can evaluate your reasoning skills and overall knowledge of psychology.

—Fourth-year public PhD student

Dissertation

No matter what type of program you're in, there's a required capstone product. Typically, this is a dissertation project that entails a comprehensive review of the literature, study conceptualization, data collection and/or analysis, and lots and lots of writing. The dissertation is the culmination of all or most of your academic skills: writing, literature analysis, sophisticated theorizing, statistics, and dissemination. It is also the development of a specialized expertise that ostensibly can springboard into a full program of independent research in the early part of your career.

Some of you will find this to be a real pleasure; others of you will find it a total drag that you just need to suffer through to get a degree. No matter what, there will likely be a proposal phase and a defense phase. I've generally found dissertation proposals to be "working meetings," where students and faculty discuss a project, scope, pragmatics, and plan to agree upon a plan. Faculty are there to help the student make choices that will result in a good product that is of sufficient quality to meet their standards. It's generally a low-stress event.

I defended my dissertation about two months after starting internship. The process was really difficult because of how daunting the whole thing felt, and how insecure I felt about my ability to produce something so long and involved, especially in the beginning. I ended up learning a lot about the subject I chose and about how I respond to certain kinds of stress, and all in all it helped with my confidence and my knowledge base. I was surprised by how good it felt to actually be done; I didn't expect it to feel like a real accomplishment, but it did.

—Seth, predoctoral intern, private PhD student

Dissertation defenses, by contrast, can feel a little less collaborative at times. Students can expect to answer tough (or tough-ish) questions about methodology, statistics, implications, and scope. I've found the questions that are asked during a dissertation defense to be on par with what might be asked of a researcher at a professional conference. The questions can be difficult, but they are also fair. And as a professor, it is a singular joy to see a student give thoughtful, well-supported, and theoretically grounded answers to faculty questions; it's a great feeling to see the emergence of a new young colleague. So, again, from the perspective of the faculty, we're not there to *grill* you (generally), but rather to give you the opportunity to show us what you know.

I imagine it must feel really rewarding to see students move through the program, gain confidence in their skills, and find success.

—Second-year private PsyD student

The most important thing I've learned is to try to reflect on why something feels like a milestone to you. Like, what part of you was motivated (or not) to try to accomplish any given thing? If it involves pure torture, definitely take the time to congratulate yourself on surviving. But in my experience, there have also been more subtle things going on behind the scenes, like need for achievement or a need to prove something. It's good to be aware of those subtleties because they can help inform future career and life decisions.

—Seth, predoctoral intern, private PhD student

On Graduation

You get one graduate school graduation.[1] The culmination of years of work, dedication, study, stress, and clinical growth gets expressed in one big ritualistic event (with robes and funny hats). All graduation ceremonies have some degree of tedium as a typically large number of students get paraded across a stage to receive a hood, a diploma, and a handshake. There's always a speaker who begins their speech with "I promise I'll keep this brief," and then proceeds to do just the opposite. An administrator or two will stand in front of your parents and friends and brag about how great the school is, and someone from the alumni organization will make a veiled request for money. All the while, you'll be anxiously waiting to hear your name called while sitting in complicated regalia that's hard to keep just in your chair.

It's easy to get jaded about this sort of thing. But you shouldn't. For all my jadedness, I'm a big believer in rituals (and robes). As a faculty member, graduation is one of my favorite days of the year because I get to welcome really wonderful and brilliant people into the profession. It's joyous. I always give students a little speech before graduation to encourage them to put any cynicism (about the process, the school, the administration, or even the choice to go to grad school!) aside and be present at a moment of transformation. If you've completed all your requirements, graduation means that by the time the ceremony is over, you get to have new letters after your name. It is a celebration of what you have done and survived, and you enter into a small and privileged group who have earned advanced degrees. It's a big responsibility, and it's a lot to be proud of. Be proud.

For many of you, graduation will require travel back from your internship sites. That's typically a big added expense on top of an already expensive process,

[1] Well, technically, if your program grants an MA/MS on the way to the doctorate, you can have two, but you know what I mean.

but I urge you to dig deep just one more time and attend your ceremony. You can also use it as an opportunity to catch up with faculty and junior colleagues. You'll really be glad you did (or your family will, which might be just as important).

· · · · · · · · · · · · · · · · · · **Words of Wisdom**   · · · · · · · · · · · · · · · ·

1. Work hard to acknowledge your successes, even if no one else notices.
2. When it comes to research, Actual Project Completion Time = 1.5 × Anticipated Project Completion Time.
3. Consider your qualifying exams as a way to demonstrate expertise.
4. For all milestones, you'll likely be more prepared than you feel like you are.

· ·

When Others Succeed and You Fail

Few things are more painful to us than the feeling of being left out or left behind. And if you're a graduate student, you're not used to failure (or perceived failure). But there may be times in graduate school when others are celebrating a success while you're nursing a wound. The juxtaposition is difficult because you want to be supportive of your colleagues, but you're grappling with feelings of insecurity, doubt, anger, or resentment. There are a few times when I typically see this situation arise: your peers' work is accepted to a conference, but yours is not; your peers pass a class, but you need to complete remedial work; your peers pass their qualifying exams, but you do not; or your peers have immediate clinical success, but your patients are floundering. All of these can be worrying and painful, but I think the biggest and hardest one for students to handle is getting passed over for an internship.

> You do you.
>
> —Fourth-year public PhD student

No matter what the *failure*, I have some general tips for coming through it relatively unscathed.

1. Remember Kübler-Ross's five stages of grief (denial, bargaining, anger, depression, and acceptance) and give yourself time to experience all of them. Don't try to talk yourself out of your feelings (e.g., "It's only an exam! I shouldn't be this upset"). Accept that you're upset and disappointed and take the time you need.
2. Determine your interpersonal resources and capacity. Some of you cope with stress by reaching out to friends and loved ones; some of you need ample alone time. There's no right way to do it, but know yourself enough to know what you need.
3. Try not to be a party pooper. If you're around others who are celebrating, do your best to bracket your disappointment. Watch yourself for sideways

expressions of anger and/or frustration that will rain on the parades of others (e.g., "You shouldn't be disappointed about your internship in [undesirable place], Carl. I mean, at least you *got* an internship"). If you're not ready to be with others, don't rush it.

4. Go into action mode as soon as you can. If there are things to be done, start the wheels turning to get them done. If you need to remediate your qualifying exams, get it finished. If you need to reboot for the second phase of the internship match, get moving on that. I once had a student who was so disappointed at having to complete qualifying exam revisions that it took him nearly *eight months* to get them done. Don't be that guy.

5. After it's all over, give it an autopsy. That is, once the dust has settled and you have some time and distance, take a step back and review what went wrong, what you learned, what warning signs you might have missed, and how you might navigate similar situations better in the future. It's true that most of our growth happens in the wake of a loss or a setback, but you need to be open to learning.

I have experienced more failures in grad school than during any other time in my life, including puberty, which says a lot. Some of them were easier to shake off, especially with normalization from peers who have gone through similar experiences. Others are more personal, and I am not really sure that I have recovered from some of them. I think a really important turning point for me in terms of the way that I've handled failures here was just to acknowledge the fact that I was surrounded by some of the most committed and intelligent people I'm ever going to meet in my life, so feelings of inadequacy are literally inevitable. Once I relinquished the expectation that I should do everything right the first time—all the time—whole new worlds of possibility opened up.

—Evelyn, fourth-year public PhD student

Dealing with failure when others are celebrating will never be easy, but knowing yourself, your colleagues, and your support system will help you successfully navigate a difficult time. And, unfortunately, those are good skills to master now, because you'll need to use them for many years to come. Who knows, maybe you might actually learn to give yourself a break from time to time and not be too hard on yourself.

Keeping Time

All APA-accredited graduate programs will inform you of their average time to completion. Nearly all programs require four years of residence followed by one year of internship. That said, many students choose to apply for internship in year five or later (about 47 percent of internship applicants in 2015; APPIC, 2015). And in fact internship match rates aren't appreciably different for those who apply in their fourth versus fifth or sixth year of grad school.[2] The point here is that there's almost no bonus for rushing through a doctoral program.

Many students come to me with some degree of anxiety about their pace through their graduate studies. As a student, you're surrounded by overachievers who are often driven to achieve, produce, and pursue all "opportunities," no matter how small. Some students can really pull off a high level of productivity, manage a personal life, and have ample downtime to binge on Netflix. But those students are the exception, not the rule (and often, there's a point of reckoning for them, too), and their high level of productivity often masks a relative lack of quality and/or depth of learning.

So, how much time should you take? In all the years that I've been a professor, I have *never* heard a student express regret at taking an additional year to complete graduate school. Not once. On the contrary, I have had a number of students who have stated that they wished they'd taken a fifth year before going to internship. Sometimes a student is forced to stay an extra year (perhaps because they did not match to an internship site, they haven't enough clinical experience, or they've not completed a departmental milestone), but the choice to stay behind is a complicated and personal one. It's not always true, but generally it seems to me that if you're considering staying for that fifth or sixth year, and the idea is not entirely repugnant to you, the answer is probably that you should.

I decided to take a fifth year because I didn't want to enter into my internship burned out before I even started. I decided that the extra year was worth my mental health, my passion, and ultimately the best opportunities to finish graduate school and begin my career in a place that I had worked so hard for.

— Predoctoral intern, private PsyD student

Like I mention above, there's *almost* no reason to rush through graduate school. However, if you attend a private school and/or have limited financial resources, the choice to stay in school another year might be cost prohibitive. Furthermore, if you have a significant other from whom you are geographically separated, you might be motivated to be as efficient as possible. All of those are good reasons, but I urge you to be kind to yourself and make a decision that is a balance of short- and long-term objectives, both personal and professional.

---

[2] Match rates are marginally higher for those who apply in their fifth or sixth year as opposed to their fourth. None of these statistics, however, take into account whether students enter a doctoral program having already completed a master's degree.

· **Tips and Strategies** · · · · · · · · · · · · · · · · · ·

1. Make time for mindful moments to notice your transitions.
2. Be clear with advisors and professors about what the expectations are. If the expectations are unclear, do what you think is best.
3. Go to your graduation!
4. Think ahead about how you will deal with perceived failures. Planful coping reduces anxiety.

You Do You

No matter what, graduate school is a ride of ups and downs, wins and losses, and successes and (perceived) failures. In the grand scheme of things, grad school is a short and intense time that will eventually merely be a distant blip in your memory. Approach it as a learner, be kind to yourself, set your own course, and take from it what you will. And in the process, attend to the moments of transformation and success, because doing so will allow for a more enriching and meaningful experience. Enjoy the journey!

Reference

Association of Psychology Postdoctoral and Internship Centers (APPIC). (2015). *2015 APPIC match: Survey of internship applicants; Part 2: Summary of applicant placement by applicant and program characteristics*. Retrieved from http://www.appic.org/Match/MatchStatistics/ApplicantSurvey2015Part2.aspx

An Anxiety-Provoking, Stress-Inducing, and Somewhat Dehumanizing Process Designed by Psychologists

The Internship Match Game

I think I started graduate school with only a vague understanding of the predoctoral internship requirement. Even if I did know about it, I'm sure that I didn't understand what a dog-and-pony show it would be to actually get one. When students enter grad school, they typically have an "I'll think about that when I need to think about it" attitude. In year two, they often enter a phase of willful ignorance. By year three, they've crossed into a more palpable dread (particularly if they're short on clinical hours). In the year of application, students generally waver between gnarly anxiety and total surrender (or they have a form of learned helplessness). Finally, after the interviews are over and the rankings submitted, many students enter a phase of calm, surrender, and excitement. It's quite the ride.

> I think I was so tired that once I submitted my rankings, I really was not that anxious because it felt so out of my control.
>
> —Predoctoral intern, private PsyD student

If you're unfamiliar with the process, it generally goes something like this: In your fourth or fifth (or twelfth) year of graduate school, you'll pick a bunch of internship sites to apply to, write a series of overly personal essays, tally and sort your clinical hours in a relatively arbitrary way, and write a separate cover letter for each site. Then, in December and January, you'll spend thousands of dollars flying all over the country, smiling politely, and meeting with psychologists and interns for interviews. You'll get sick at least once. You'll sleep on at least one couch, spend time with a relative you really don't like, and have at least one wardrobe problem. You'll drain your bank account (or those of your relatives). You'll learn about how you manage (or don't) your anxiety over a prolonged period of time. At the end of this quest, you'll submit an ordered list of sites to an online ranking system and then sit in quiet, anxious rumination for a few weeks during which no one can talk to one another. Then voila! You'll check your email and find out where you'll be moving in a few months. Alternatively, you'll find out that you didn't match anywhere, and you'll quickly reboot for the second phase of the match, where unmatched students and internships make deals and hopefully find homes for one another. Sounds like a great time, right?

Applying for internship seems to be the hazing process of the professional psychologists' world. It is unnecessarily expensive, complex, and stressful. The mixed messages about the weight and importance of this transformative year while trying to assuage the uncertainty and Harry Potter sorting hat match process felt confusing and challenging.

—Michelle, fourth-year private PsyD student

I can assure you that this process is better than it used to be. In the long, long time ago period, the whole thing was a lot more chaotic and often unfair because internships could make offers at any point in order to scoop up the best interns. Students would often hold multiple offers, leaving other students to scramble at the last minute. Internships then often lost the chance to make offers to other students. The computer matching process has cleaned things up a lot, as have the communication rules between students and internships.

In the more recent long ago period, the internship matching process was even more gnarly because of the sizable *match imbalance*. That is, there were far more students looking for internships than there were internships available. Through the efforts of APA and APPIC (Association of Psychology Postdoctoral and Internship Centers), the match imbalance is less imbalanced. Although a number of students still go unmatched each year (particularly those from unaccredited doctoral programs), a lack of internships is less a matter of concern than it used to be.

There are lots of good books and resources out there to help you navigate the process (APAGS [the American Psychological Association of Graduate Students] has a number of them), so I'm not going to belabor you with pragmatics. My goal here is just to help you know what to expect and what the process is actually like (hint: it's better than you think it'll be). I've been a director of clinical training for eight years in two different programs, so I'm pretty well acquainted with the process.

One thing to remember is that graduate school is not merely preparation for internship; it's preparation for your life and career. Internship is just another step along the journey. It's the last step of your graduate school career and an extension of your career trajectory (if you have one). My advice to students is to remember that internship is a means to an end, not an end in itself. Prepare for life, not for internship. With that in mind, let's march through some of the decision points and milestones.

Am I Ready to Apply?

How should I know? I don't even know you!

OK, so maybe that's not helpful. In my mind, there are a couple of things to consider in making this decision. First, do you have enough clinical experience? Students are often obsessed with clinical *hours* despite the fact that internship directors often say that such raw numbers are relatively unimportant (APPIC, 2017). Your focus should be on the depth of your experience and how that experience matches your desired career. If you have 2,000 hours working with children with autism but you want a career in a college counseling center, you're pretty screwed. The number of hours is not as important as their relevance to the sites you'll apply to. Internships need to know that they can put you to work doing something as soon as you get there (other than sweeping up). In consultation with your director of clinical training (DCT) or internship advisor, you can decide whether you have the depth and breadth of experience needed to apply for internship.

The other major consideration is the status of your dissertation. As I mentioned earlier in the book, not having a completed dissertation during internship is a real nightmare. Most programs these days require students to at least propose their dissertations prior to applying for internship (and most internships require this step too). I'd go one step further: Even if you have proposed your dissertation, if you don't think that you can make *significant* headway toward completing it prior to starting internship, I would urge you to think seriously about staying back a year to finish. Your internship year is a prized year of full-time training. It's exhausting both physically and emotionally. Having to wrestle with dissertation stuff in the evenings without a research advisor around is a real drag, and you run the risk of completing your internship but having to delay graduation by a semester or quarter in order to finish up afterward. I've seen enough students get derailed by this that I feel pretty strongly about it. If you can at all afford it, it's better to take an extra year and get the project done than it is to flounder after internship to slap something together.

Site Selection

How do you know which sites to pick? Again, the thing to remember is that it's a match. If there's not a clean match between your experiences, your goals, and a site's training opportunities, it doesn't matter how prepared you are—you

FIGURE 8.1. How to think about site selection.

won't get matched. There should be some overlap between what they need you to do and what you can do, but the overlap shouldn't be total. That is, they need something to teach you, and you need something that you can do for them (see figure 8.1).

It surprised me how long it took to review all the sites I might be interested in.
— Dee, fourth-year private PsyD student

Our program is incredibly supportive. They guide you through every step of the process and provide excellent feedback along the way. That said, it sometimes felt like their support had ulterior motives. I don't doubt that our program cares a great deal about our well-being, but at times it seemed like the outcome statistics of the program took priority. I found myself questioning whether recommendations on site selection were genuinely based on my interests and goals, or if they were more in line with wanting to increase the program's match rate.
— Fourth-year private PsyD student

I'll avoid discussion of having "safety" sites and "reachy" sites, but I think it's fair to remind you that the biggest killer of a successful match is geographic restrictions. I understand the importance of family and love (see Chapter 1), but if you live in a competitive area like California, Chicago, or the northeastern corridor, it'll behoove you to apply to a handful of sites in other, less competitive locations. In the end, it's a year. It's a year in which you could have a different experience that broadens your horizons. I don't think students should apply to places where they don't feel safe or their race, religion, sexual orientation, or gender expression might put them at risk, but, those considerations aside, I suggest that all students reach a bit in terms of places they'd be willing to go to finish their degree.

I picked sites based on the types of clinical and research experiences offered. I wanted places where they were doing work similar to what I had done before, but could still offer me a valuable learning and training experience. I also wanted sites that were more in line with my theoretical orientation and approach (but I was still open to learning new ones).

—Erin, fourth-year public PhD student

To be honest, I was a lot less methodical when selecting which sites I would apply to than I should have been. One of my "tiers" was "geographical locations where I'd actually want to end up" (i.e., near friends and family). So I definitely applied to a few of those, but since geographical restriction is such a big no-no, I tried to deliberately pick a few sites that were in places that seemed like they would be undesirable as "destination sites" on a geographical level, but some of those turned out to be unexpectedly really competitive! I did rely a lot on the little APPIC equation to determine the site's competitivity record, and I was definitely stunned and disheartened by how competitive some sites were that I had never heard of. I tried to avoid applying to too many sites that were under 4 percent acceptance rate, but realistically almost all of the ones that fit my criteria for specialty area/supervision approach/and training opportunities were around 2–3 percent, which was demoralizing.

—Evelyn, fourth-year public PhD student

I tried to find a balance between location and training. Although I didn't apply to any sites in locations that I wouldn't be comfortable living in for a year, I did apply to sites that were far away if the training was a great match for my goals. I also applied to a handful of sites that were in an ideal location, even if the training wasn't a perfect match.

—Teal, fourth-year private PsyD student

The Essays

As of this writing, there are four essays required for the application. These 500-word essays are about your theoretical orientation, your ability to consider diversity, your research achievements and goals, and an autobiographical statement. Five hundred words isn't a lot (it's about one typewritten page), so you need to be clear, dense, and precise (and creative, interesting, thoughtful, and deep). Of these, the autobiographical statement is generally seen as the most important, and students find it the most difficult to write.

Writing an autobiographical statement was the hardest essay. To condense a lifetime of experiences into 500 words and have a cohesive, yet professional, narrative is impossible. The nature of the task seems to overly simplify the beautiful complexity of people, let alone psychology grad students who seem to be even more complex. Ultimately, I wrote many drafts for the many versions of myself and tried to take some pieces from each one.

—Michelle, fourth-year private PsyD student

How do you capture yourself in a 500-word essay? Students seem to struggle with how personal, how professional, how disclosing, and how formal to be. In my experience, the essay should be a bit more personal than you might expect. Unlike the essays you write to get into graduate school, if your statement is merely a recounting of how much you loved your psychology classes and want to help people, you're not likely to get many interviews. Internship directors need to know that you have insight and self-knowledge and the reasons you want to be a psychologist. It might take some soul-searching to find those *real* answers, but that's an important part of the process. There have been lots of times that a student has come to me with a new insight about themselves and their past just from writing their essays. It's heady stuff.

I was not able to find a way to write an autobiographical statement that did not sound contrived or cheesy, and I really did try. Even though this is true of most of the (written and in-person) materials of internship applications to some extent, finding that balance between "make it sincere and memorable and unique . . . but don't be a TMI weirdo!" was difficult to strike. I think it just inevitably conjures up a lot of self-consciousness to be put on the spot with this type of question, and I have a lot of respect for people who are actually able to be appropriately open and honest in their autobiographical statement.

—Evelyn, fourth-year public PhD student

The autobiographical statement feels like a trap. How do you possibly summarize your life story in 500 words in a way that makes you seem compelling, competent, and likeable to complete strangers? How do you bridge the gap between being professional but also personal?

—Predoctoral intern, public PhD student

The other three essays are generally easier to write. In completing these essays, students often rely on tips from older students who have successfully matched. Compared to the autobiographical statement, these essays generally feel a little formulaic. The only advice I'd offer here is that there should not be redundancy across the essays. My friend and former colleague Dr. Kimberly Hill says that the four essays should be like four chapters in a book. They should fit together to form a coherent professional narrative of who you are, how you think, how you practice, and what your interests are. The four essays can't tell the *entire* story, but they can tell an *interesting* one.

I thought it was weird to write the diversity statement. As a student of color, and someone who focuses on multicultural competence, it was hard to say everything I wanted to say in so little space. In a way, it felt that I was bragging about being a POC, something completely outside my control.

—Fifth-year public PhD student

It felt like there was more of a "right" answer to the diversity statement. I would imagine that the majority of applicants say something along the lines of "Diversity is important. Here is how I worked with diverse clients, and yet I am always striving to be more culturally competent." As a result, it was hard to know how to stand out from other applicants in this essay.

—Teal, fourth-year private PsyD student

The most helpful advice that I received on the theoretical orientation essay was that it was OK if it was messy. It felt sadistic of them to ask us to sum this up in such a short space, and realistically, as someone who does integrate a lot of different theoretical and technical approaches into my clinical work, it felt like I was lying in some way to try to only pick a couple in order to maintain some compositional cogency.

—Evelyn, fourth-year public PhD student

I enjoyed writing my research statement tremendously just as I have enjoyed all of my research activities over the years. This was easy to write about because research is something we frequently talk about with each other without any reservations. I'm used to talking about my research with colleagues and faculty in the lab, in the classroom, and at conferences. I haven't had the same opportunities to talk about my life story, my theoretical orientation (who even has one anymore?), or my experience with diversity.

—Predoctoral intern, private PsyD student

Finally, be prepared for multiple drafts. Although I have tips and strategies for each essay that I provide my students (and I'm sure your DCT has the same), the best and simplest advice is to get started early (early being the summer beforehand). An early start allows you to write a draft, let it sit, and then revisit it with fresh eyes. If you're lucky enough to have a program that helps with editing, make sure that you've done your diligence before passing it along to someone else.

Our program provided internship coaches who helped read over our CVs, cover letters, essays, and site lists, as well as provide strategy.

—Michelle, fourth-year private PsyD student

I thought that my program was fairly supportive until I learned how much support students had in other programs. We had a few meetings throughout the process, whereas other programs provided their students with a lot more support. Many programs had entire classes devoted to preparing students for internship applications.

—Predoctoral intern, public PhD student

My program provided a substantial amount of support over the course of a couple of years leading up to applications in the form of course work, a dedicated advisor for internship, and resources from students who have applied in the past. I have had three people, faculty and students, read through all of my materials. I have had constant email communications, with recommended timelines, general updates, and other how-tos, from my program's office of professional development to help keep me on track. I have had meetings with my internship advisor, who has read several drafts of all my materials and provided valuable feedback on everything from my site list to my CV. The database of application, interview, and match data from all of the students from my program who have applied in the past was a great resource to find sites and refine my site list.

—Fourth-year private PhD student

Interviews (or How to Look Chill in an Uncomfortable Polyester Suit)

After you submit your materials to sites, you'll be contacted for interviews pretty quickly. Increasingly, sites are interviewing in early to late December. This means that you shouldn't pick this particular winter break to take a trip to Iceland. One of the most chaotic parts of interviewing is scheduling them. Sites often have only a handful of set interview days, which means that you might need to schedule, rearrange, and schedule again. When it's time to schedule interviews, try to schedule your most prized sites toward the middle of your interview trip. Remember again the Yerkes-Dodson curve: you'll be really nervous for your first few interviews, but by the end, you won't care anymore. There's a sweet spot there in the middle where you're still a little anxious, but you still care. That sweet spot is where you want to be for your top choices.

Interviewing is the worst! It's exhausting! You have to fly all over the country, and you get almost no sleep. Eighteen interviews in a month is way too many! By the end, I was considering switching to an entirely different field altogether.

—Predoctoral intern, public PhD student

Provided that you're not a huge pain in the neck about it,[1] you can call a site to reschedule an interview to make travel plans easier. There's also no need to be coy about the fact that you have other interviews; just let them know that you have a conflict and ask them whether they can work with you. Of course, if you're applying to predominantly college counseling sites, scheduling is a little easier because most of them do phone or video interviews (somehow college counseling centers are the only sites that have gotten the memo that grad students have no money).

Another practical word of advice: Get a flu shot. Travel plus fatigue equals sickness. Sickness plus interviews equals sadness. Don't be sad.

One thing that often surprises students is how fun the interview process is. Yes, it's exhausting, but it's also a great experience. You get to travel to interesting places, meet real-life psychologists doing interesting work, imagine different career trajectories, and have great conversations about psychology with interesting people. You'll be surprised at how much you know and how well prepared you'll be. I generally find that students return with a greater sense of agency and efficacy after their round of internship interviews.

At some sites I instantly felt welcomed, calm, and put at ease by the people interviewing me. At others, I felt nervous, uncomfortable, and like I had no idea what I was doing. Those feelings ended up being one of the ways I made my rankings later on.

—Predoctoral intern, private PsyD student

The best part about interviewing is that you meet certain people whom you see at a number of different sites along the way. It creates a certain camaraderie. I had a group chat with a few people I met at my first interview that we kept

---

[1] Seriously, don't be a pain in the neck or impolite to anyone, particularly the program staff. I've heard stories of applications getting "lost" because a student was rude to a staff member. Program staff make the program run, so never underestimate how important they are to the training directors. Plus, you should just never be rude to anyone no matter the context. Your mom taught you that, right?

going throughout the interview process. On match day, we all texted to celebrate where we all ended up. It was really nice to have people to talk to who
understood the process and were going through the same thing simultaneously.

—Predoctoral intern, public PhD student

I meet people on the interview trail with whom I still keep in touch, and I like
that I learned a lot about different ways people provide mental health care—for
better and for worse.

—Predoctoral intern, public PhD student

One thing that's not surprising is how exhausting it is. Airplanes, trains,
rental cars, hotels, couches, reading materials, regretting answers you gave, and
smiling politely all add up to a lot of fatigue. When I interviewed, I was on the
road for three weeks, bouncing around the Northeast and Midwest, crashing
on couches and in cheap hotels. By the end, I was pretty trashed and ready to
get home. Be sure that your winter quarter/semester workload is a light one
because I guarantee you won't feel like keeping up with class readings during
interviews, and you won't be too excited to catch up when you come back.
Prepare for being an exhausted mess.

It took a lot more energy than I anticipated. The prepping, traveling, researching
the places, being "on," having to talk to people and be socially appropriate for
so long. I would get home exhausted!

—Predoctoral intern, public PhD student

As you might imagine, this whole process is not designed for the bank ac-
counts of poor graduate students. In 2016, the median dollar amount spent
by students on the entire process was $1,800 (including application fees and
travel). This expense does not include wardrobe updates or the opportunity cost
of not being able to work another job during the time you're traveling. My advice is to start a savings account early on in your graduate career and deposit
a little money into it each month for your internship expenses. Fifty bucks a
month for 36 months will yield $1,800. I understand that $50 might be hard
(or impossible) to come by, but, no matter what, stashing a little away is always
better than scrambling to come up with big bucks in one large chunk.

The Match

In February, you'll be back from your interviews and trying to resume your normal
life. You can't have any contact with internships at that point, but you still need
to rank order the sites where you applied. I typically find that students are pretty
sure about their first choices and their last choices; it's the in-between sites that
are harder to rank. You must weigh location, training, opportunities for partners,

and availability of postdocs. There are a lot of considerations, and everyone has a unique profile of needs and wants. Talk it all through with someone you trust.

About two weeks after you submit your rankings, you'll get an email on match day telling you where you've matched. The match is a contract, so once you've submitted your ranking, you've agreed to show up and work where you match. I've always found match day to be a real blast; how often do you get a simple email that will possibly change your life? It's often cause for celebration and, more palpably, relief. Indeed, in 2016, 73 percent of students were matched to their first- or second-choice internship (APPIC, 2017).

Of course, some students don't get matched in the first round. This is often a matter of statistics and poor site selection rather than a reflection on the quality or preparation of a student. Luckily, the second phase of the match is a relatively humane process where students can reapply to open positions that might be good matches. And don't think that unfilled internships are somehow of poorer quality; several really high-quality internships have unfilled spots each year. I have placed several students in internships during the second phase that they absolutely loved. Alternatively, if a student does not match, they can choose to hang out for a year and work on strengthening their application for the following year.

· · · · · · · · · · · · · · · · · · **Words of Wisdom** · · · · · · · · · · · · · · · · · · ·

1. Prepare for your life, not your internship.
2. Think about your professional narrative throughout your time in graduate school.
3. Plan to be anxious during the application and interview months. Think ahead about what you'll do to take care of yourself.

· ·

Friends and Family

No matter what the process is like for you, it's nearly impossible for friends and family to get their heads around. When you describe the process to someone who isn't in the field (and who isn't a physician, because their residency match process is similar), it sounds completely bananas. If you have a partner or family who will be moving with you, this process is even more daunting for them because they don't have any control over what happens. All of these pressures can put students in a bind between wanting what's best for their training and what might be preferable for their friends and family. In those moments, it's important to be as clear as possible about what it is that you want and what choices might lead to resentment or discord.

I think my friends and family have had a hard time understanding the match process in general. They keep thinking that I will be getting multiple "offers" and will get to choose from them. In particular, my partner had a hard time understanding why I would want to apply to a site in an undesirable city. I had to explain and reexplain that it was a match, so by limiting the geographic location, I was limiting my chance to match. It took some time, but he eventually realized that the program's fit with my interests and goals is what matters more than where it is.

—Erin, fourth-year public PhD student

To make it to the level of earning a doctorate degree, most of us had to be organized planners. Having complete lack of control over my (and my partner's) future has been challenging. I found that not avoiding the topic and talking it out (over several months) finally allowed us to get on the same page. I was prepared for my partner to give his input into what sites I applied to, but when that time came, he fully understood how little control I had over the final outcome and was supportive of wherever I chose to apply. After all, it's only one year!

—Amy, fourth-year public PhD student

My friends and family outside of psychology thought the process was crazy. My mom even mentioned that it was ironic that it was designed by psychologists.

—Predoctoral intern, public PhD student

I think it's been pretty rare that people outside of the field really grasp how intensive the internship application process is for us, and I feel like a jerk for complaining about it all the time to them because there are obviously an infinite number of worse things in life than being in a position to apply for a predoctoral internship. So I try to save most of my complaints for other people who are going though the process, since commiseration really can be helpful, in my experience. One thing that I did start doing per the wise advice of a recently licensed faculty member is just describing it as a "residency year," since this is a term with which many more people are familiar. Otherwise, I definitely get the impression that they think of the generic image of "internship" and assume that I'm applying to fetch somebody's latte and make copies for a year, and they can't understand why I am so stressed about it.

—Evelyn, fourth-year public PhD student

Angst

For nearly all students, the internship application process is an anxiety riddled experience. The lack of control coupled with an uncertain fate is a gnarly calculus. The fact that it's a relatively protracted period usually starting in June and running through mid-March makes it even worse. To be clear, *most students get one of their top choices*, but given that most doctoral students are accustomed to being able to control, predict, or manage their futures, it can be a new and uncomfortable experience. This anxiety leads students to second-guess their work in a way they typically might not and to worry about outcomes they can't control. The process of applying for internship is not difficult, but the weight of anxiety makes it seem harder than it really is.

I have struggled with anxiety my whole life, so I knew this would be a triggering event for me. The best way I was able to cope was to break down tasks into smaller ones, so I felt more accomplished with each check on my to-do list. I also made every attempt to integrate self-care, which for me was exercise and spending time with loved ones. I would schedule in application work time into my calendar, and I kept pretty strict about it so that I was not spending excessive time on this one aspect of my life.

—Erin, fourth-year public PhD student

Anxiety during internship applications is unprecedented by other graduate school activities. I was not nearly this anxious about my comprehensive exams or even my dissertation proposal. The abundance of unknowns in the process of applying for internships has wreaked havoc on me, but I am coping by spending as much time as I can with people outside the internship world and outside psychology.

—Fifth-year private PhD student

My anxiety came in waves during the application process. In the very early stages, I felt pretty confident. That confidence quickly faded, though, when I looked at the APPIC directory profiles of sites and realized how fantastic and qualified the applicants from previous years have been. I noticed myself getting really caught up in the details, like the number of integrated reports or publications I have compared to previous applicants. Surprisingly, writing the cover letters actually helped to decrease my anxiety. I had to shift my focus back to my own experiences, rather than comparing myself to other applicants. Looking over my CV, my hours, and many other aspects of my applications actually made me feel pretty accomplished! I have also found it very helpful to reach out to students in years above me who have been through the process. They often have great perspective on the application process as a whole.

—Teal, fourth-year private PsyD student

It's clear that, during the internship application year, you need to be diligent about taking care of yourself and pampering your relationships. Like saving money, having self-care resources and routines in place throughout your time in grad school will serve you well when the application year comes around. If you have a routine of exercise, pottery, James Bond movie watching, or "foot massage Wednesdays," then you won't need to scramble to find what works when/if you get angsty during the weeks when you're writing 18 cover letters.

It's also fair to warn your relatives and loved ones that you might be less available (emotionally and physically) for a handful of months so that they don't feel entirely shut out.

On Internshipping

All the angst-related energy is an investment in the last year of your training. Internship is and should be a culmination of your clinical training thus far. It's a full year of intense clinical work with lots of supervision, didactics, and friendships with fellow interns from all over the country. It's likely the most independent you'll be and when you'll really feel like other psychologists are treating you like a colleague rather than just a student. I've found that nearly all students really love their internship year (I know I did).

During school you had a lot of different aspects, including class, practicum, homework, and applications, but you basically got to control when and where you worked on a majority of those things. Internship is much less like that, and I find that while I'm working about the same number of hours, it feels like more because I can't take a break and go to the gym and then come back and do more work.

—Predoctoral intern, private PsyD student

The most challenging thing about internship is that it is a year of learning, which in turn means it is a year of not knowing and frequently feeling incompetent or unsure.

—Predoctoral intern, public PhD student

Internship is so much better than graduate school! Instead of having three jobs, you only have the one. You get to devote all of your time to developing your skills as a clinician. It's also the first time in five years that I've taken an entire weekend off.

—Predoctoral intern, public PhD student

No matter what your internship experience, you'll likely emerge as more confident, more professional, and more independent in your role as a psychologist. It's likely that you'll get even more clarity on your career objectives, and it's also probable that you'll see your graduate school years in a new light. The change in graduate students from the beginning of internship to the end of internship is palpable, and I'm always amazed at how much change and growth happens during that year. Savor as much of it as you can.

· · · · · · · · · · · · · · · · · Tips and Strategies · · · · · · · · · · · · · · · ·

1. Track your clinical hours as soon as you start graduate school. Really. Do it.
2. Start the site selection and essay-writing processes as soon as you can.
3. Make significant headway on your dissertation. If you don't think you can finish it by the time you start internship, seriously consider taking another year.
4. Get a flu shot.
5. Save a little money each month you're in school to offset interview and application expenses. Even a few bucks will make a big difference to your future self.

· ·

The internship application year can be a long and lonely one with a million choice points. It's a process that will force you to reflect on who you are, why you're becoming a psychologist, and what it is you'd like to do with your life and your career. A year from when you start the process, you'll end up living in a different place, and you'll have new and different colleagues. You'll need to manage a fair amount of anxiety and discomfort, but the reward is well worth it. You'll emerge as a competent and confident psychologist and fulfill the final requirement of your degree (provided that you finished your stupid dissertation). And you'll be one step closer to the career you've finally started to see clearly.

Reference

Association of Psychology Postdoctoral and Internship Centers (APPIC). (2017). *2016 APPIC match: Survey of internship applicants; Part 1: Summary of survey results.* Retrieved from https://www.appic.org/Match/Match-Statistics/Applicant-Survey-2016-Part-1

CHAPTER 9

Going Pro
Becoming a Human Psychologist

66 **W**hat do you want to do with your life?" It's probably the question that I ask graduate students the most often. If you're like me, you'll enter graduate school with a particular idea or vision about what you want to do with your career but leave with at least a marginally altered plan. When I went to graduate school, my ultimate plan was to teach at a small private liberal arts college and work with kids in the juvenile justice system. I've done a lot of things in my career, but I've neither taught at a small liberal arts college nor worked with kids in the juvenile justice system. Things change.

> Since starting graduate school, I'm even more interested in teaching as an adjunct professor in addition to practicing full time as a psychologist.
>
> —Natassia, second-year private PhD student

> Absolutely, my interests have changed since I started grad school. I've found my clinical interests have changed drastically, but my research interests have stayed in the same area but grown in depth.
>
> —Stephanie, fifth-year public PhD student

Although things change, the "What do you want to do with your life?" question is always a relevant one. There are a couple of ways of looking at graduate school. On one hand, it's a means to an end: you go to learn skills and abilities that will serve you in your career. That is, it's training toward a particular end. The other way to look at it is an end in and of itself: you go to learn things that are of interest to you, regardless of their practical value. That is, the education is the end in itself. I'd argue that each of these perspectives is partly correct: psychology graduate school is both a means and an end.

The balance of your time between means and end will have implications for the choices you make. If you lean more toward the *means* side, your training might be pretty narrow, focused only on one or two things (e.g., eating disorders, assessment, adolescents). If you lean more toward the *end* side, your training might be so broad that you don't develop any depth of knowledge or experience. Neither of those extremes is likely to serve you well. As psychologists, we need a broad array of experience to draw upon, but we also need some areas where we really know our stuff and feel a certain sense of expertise.

All of this means that you'll need to make some decisions during your time in graduate school. Time is a nonrenewable and limited commodity, so there will be opportunities that you will need to skip. So how do you manage the competing pressures of breadth and depth? First, let me confess a personal bias: I'm a fan of generalist training during grad school (with specialized training during postdoc and maybe internship). That is, I think students should seek broad training and not hem themselves into a specialization too early in training. People are really complicated, and the more perspectives you've had on humanness, the better (in my opinion). This does not mean that you should have no areas of particular interest (because you should), but rather that you should expose yourself to more than just one or two areas of focus.

Be open to change. Be open to being wrong. Be open to asking questions.

—Natassia, second-year private PhD student

So, what do you want to do with your life? It's likely that you have a vision of what you want your career to look like. Private practice? Public school district? Research university? Group practice? Water ski instructor? Hospital? Veterans Affairs center? Consultation? Supervision? Liberal arts college? Assessment psychologist? Policy wonk? None of the above? With an MA degree in psychology, you'll have many options; with a doctorate, you'll have many more. A graduate student once said to me, "I'm not exactly sure what I want to do because I'm pretty sure that it's not a thing yet." You should always have the flexibility to drastically change course along the way, but even a broad and general starting vision of what you think you'd like to do will be helpful (even if it's "none of the above").

My colleague Dr. Miya Barnett advises students to start reading job ads in their first year of graduate school. By reading ads for the types of jobs you might want, you can see what qualifications they're looking for, and then you can gain experience accordingly. If you want to be a university professor, then learning how to publish and apply for grants should be a priority; if you want to be a clinical neuropsychologist, then be prepared for a two-year postdoc. Knowing soon what you need to get to the place you want to be will help you design a graduate school experience that suits your needs.

By the time you apply for internships and jobs, you'll need to have crafted a professional narrative. Essentially, you'll need a story of your training and how all of your experiences have fit together (or not). You'll need to craft a story of what it is you know and what it is you don't know. For example, my early professional narrative was that I did assessment and I worked with kids (and I did assessment with kids). My clinical experience and my research were generally either kid related or assessment related. Although I had this narrative of being an assessment kid guy, I had lots of experience with adults too. So even as you begin your graduate training, think about the narrative you'd like to craft, recognize that it will change drastically (and that's OK!), and seek experiences that add to (or expand) that narrative.

It's scary but exciting at the same time to develop a specialty area. There are so many interesting rabbit holes that one can go down. It's difficult to decide which to give more of your energy to.

—Natassia, second-year private PhD student

Remember, however, that your narrative is merely a story to guide your training toward a particular career objective or internship type. It is not a set of prison bars that hold you in to one thing for the rest of your life. Research tells us that the half-life of a degree in psychology is about eight years (Neimeyer, Taylor, Rozensky, & Cox, 2014), meaning that half of what you learn in graduate school will be out of date in about eight years. Given that what you learn in psychology will eventually be out of date, the *real* thing you're learning is *how to learn* psychology and *how to think* like a psychology professional. Graduate school gives you tools to learn, and those are far more important than the individual *facts* and *truths* that you're learning now (because those will change). In my career, I've been trained as a clinical neuropsychologist and published on behavior rating scales, the Rorschach, and therapeutic models of assessment. I've worked with kids in bereavement and kids with medical illnesses, and I've spent time as the consulting psychologist to a Division I department of athletics. Now I specialize in the psychological needs of boys and men and give talks on healthy sport participation for kids and mindfulness in business. Most of what I do now I never could have dreamed of in graduate school, but as I've continued to shift and grow in my interests, I've used the lessons of graduate school on how to learn things (e.g., visiting the literature, talking to more experienced people, getting supervision). Things will change for you too, and you'll be well equipped to learn what you need to.

It's difficult if your interests change, and you feel a lot of pressure to focus on one specific thing. But that doesn't seem reasonable. I tried to get as much variety as I could in my research and externships as not to be boxed into one tiny area. This often meant reaching out to other faculty and trying to piece different interests together to make one coherent interest.

—Third-year private PhD student

"No" Is Not a Four-Letter Word

Let's face it—if you're a graduate student (or potential graduate student), you're probably lousy at saying no to things. You've probably done really well by saying yes to any and all opportunities, even if it meant that you had to be extra tired, grumpy, or broke. If you're an older student with a family of your own, you might have developed your no muscle to some degree already, but many of you will be in relatively uncharted territory with no. I *still* have a lot of trouble with no. But no is our friend.

Saying no is really difficult. You have to do it to maintain your own sanity and well-being, but at the same time, every time you say no, there's this tiny voice in your head that worries that by saying no you've just let everyone know you're an imposter who doesn't deserve to be in grad school because you can't juggle seventeen things like *insert name of anyone else in your cohort*. But you have to ignore that voice, because trust me, there has never been a time where I felt overwhelmed and said no and came to regret it.

—Second-year public PhD student

Remember that you need to craft a personal narrative that fits your career goals. But you also need to be a teamplayer who pitches in to help others, and you need to have a few experiences that might be outside of your scope of developing expertise. Deciding how and when to say no is a tricky calculus because you'll need to weigh personal and professional relationships, your own state of mental capacity, and any plans for personal time and self-care. Here are a few questions to consider in the yes/no decision:

1. Does the opportunity fit with your long-term career goals and professional narrative?
2. Does the opportunity help a student colleague who has helped you (or who might do so in the future)?
3. Will the opportunity slow down your progress in completing research projects?
4. Have you been a big slacker and not chipped in before?
5. What is the relationship like with the person offering the opportunity? Are they likely to retaliate or hold a grudge?
6. If you say yes, will you be resentful and angry such that you won't do a good job?
7. Will the opportunity pull you away from time with your family, friends, or romantic partners?
8. Will the opportunity expose you to a population, problem, or methodology that you find interesting?
9. Are you overextended already?
10. How much sleep did you get last night, anyway?

Certainly, there are more questions to be asked, but this is a good start.

It's been scary to say no to things because I wonder what I am missing out on. However, I remember that I can't do everything and be everywhere no matter how hard I try. It's difficult to make choices because I don't want to miss out on anything that could be helpful along the road, but it's like driving down a foggy road. You don't know where you're going until you get there.

—Natassia, second-year private PhD student

The tyranny of choice is real. This is where a helpful mentor comes in and/ or supportive senior students—I found it extremely helpful to shoot senior lab mates an email when I was questioning if a training opportunity was worth the time/financial cost.

—Fifth-year public PhD student

A judicious use of no and yes will help you navigate the opportunities available in grad school and will manage everyone's expectations of you. As a professor, I really like students who say yes at least part or most of the time. And the more a student says yes, the more I tend to ask them to do (even when I shouldn't). Saying yes translates to a perception of reliability. But students who *always* say yes tend to come to a point of reckoning eventually. Practice saying no now because it will serve you well in the long run. I've ended up saying yes to things that I didn't really want to do. I ended up feeling resentful, and the quality of things that I really wanted to do broke down. Practice saying no with grace. No is our friend.

Once you become a part of this community, you get emails left and right about trainings on this or that. It all depends on what you put your energy toward. I feel like I can explore anything I want to. Time management is always an issue, but other than that, other professionals are very generous with their time and knowledge.

—Second-year private PhD student

· · · · · · · · · · · · · · · · · **Words of Wisdom** · · · · · · · · · · · · · · · · · ·

1. Learning to say no is a life skill.
2. Consider having a specialty area, but don't be hemmed into just one thing.
3. Picture your future life and arrange training to get you there.
4. It's OK to change interests as you learn more and your career develops.

Being You, Being Professional

In the second or third year of graduate school, I tend to see a transformation in students. They begin to shift from *students* to *professionals*. Although they're professionals in training, there's a discernible difference in carriage and an increase in personal directedness and responsibility. It's cool because I can see the emergence of a future colleague. But hopefully they're still the same people they were before. Like becoming yourself as a clinician, graduate school will challenge you to become yourself as a professional.

I can be myself only to a certain point . . . can't let out all of myself. These professors are always watching you. They're intrusive. I know it's all for my betterment, but it's unsettling at times.

—Second-year private PhD student

What does it mean to be a professional? Does it mean that you'll need to wear a lot of polyester and uncomfortable shoes? Does being a professional mean that you need to be oddly formal and uptight? Does it mean that you need to be bland and generic? Does it mean that you need to get rid of your sweet eyebrow ring? Maybe, but not necessarily. And the answers to those questions will be different at the beginning of your career than after you're established, they'll depend on where you work and where you live, and they will be different given who you are and how you're likely to be perceived.

Knowing that my personal identity is still evolving is the hardest part of blending my personal and professional identities. I think I know who I am one minute and then the other minute, I feel lost. My professional identity feels more set in stone.

—Second-year private PhD student

One way to potentially break down professionalism is in terms of professional behavior and professional attitudes. APA's Competency Benchmarks describe such behaviors as professional communication, appropriate dress, and accepting responsibility for your actions. Professional attitudes include honesty, ethics, a desire to protect the welfare of others, having the identity of a psychologist, and integrating science and practice.

OK, so what does that mean? A few examples of professional behaviors follow:

1. Come to class and appointments on time and be attentive.
2. Dress well without being too formal, too casual, too weird, or even remotely sexy.
3. Respond to emails within a maximum of 48 hours (24 hours is recommended), unless you're camping or on a ship at sea or something. And if you're camping or at sea, have a vacation responder.
4. Greet psychologists as Dr. So-and-So until either (a) you've been invited to call them otherwise or (b) you become Dr. So-and-So too.
5. Don't have a goofy email address. It's time to retire imafraidofclowns@hotmail.com.
6. When emailing faculty or other professionals, use complete sentences and proper punctuation, but keep it short.
7. Know your way around PsychINFO and do thoughtful and thorough literature searches on things of interest, issues that your clients have, treatment approaches, and so forth.

8. Even when not in a professional setting, remember how you appear to others. Assume that you will run into a client, a student in a class you're teaching, or a professor. If you have a tendency to be obnoxious in public, it's probably best to curb that sort of thing now. Your days of going nuts at the club are probably over (unless you're out of town). And never, ever talk about your clients in a place where you can be overheard. Even if you're not discussing details, you can do a great deal of damage to the public trust in psychotherapy by making it seem normal for therapists to be talking about clients in public.

9. Go on social media lockdown. Boost all of your privacy settings, get rid of incriminating online photos, and consider using an alias for all your personal online activities. This is not true for all professions, but given that we work with the public in positions of trust with vulnerable populations, we need to be extra careful. No one wants to see pictures of their therapist boozin' it up in Vegas (and if you think your clients aren't searching for you online, you're mistaken). And, as an aside, never search for your clients online (unless you check it with your supervisor first).

10. Remember that there's a hierarchy, and your position as a graduate student is near the bottom. I think it's important that you advocate for yourself, but it's important that you do so with respect and humility. Arrogance (or the perception of arrogance) is a real kiss of death.

11. Be true to your word. If you say that you'll have it done by Friday, have it done by Friday. If you say that you'll help out, help out. If you can't deliver on what you've promised, be up front about that in plenty of time.

As a student from an underrepresented group and the first in my family to attend college and graduate school, I don't think I could have made it this far without my undergraduate mentor, who has a PhD in clinical psychology. She has been my most significant mentor and has long been a model for what it means to be a psychologist and to wear multiple hats (researcher, clinician, teacher, mentor) in a professional and ethical way. She has been my model in what a fulfilling career in psychology can look like and has inspired me to keep pushing forward even when the road looked bleak.

—Stephanie, fifth-year public PhD student

Of course, what it means to be professional is partly a function of who you are and how you're likely to be perceived. Because I'm a White man, the barriers to my success have been much lower than for those of you who are of a minority or underrepresented group. It's a sad truth that many of you will have to overcome systemic barriers, racism, ageism, sexism, and both implicit and explicit biases of others. For my entire career, I've been able to get away with being relatively informal even while being perceived as professional. Many of you will not have that luxury. I like to think that psychology is better than other fields, but there is still a long way to go and we're not there yet. As I noted in Chapter 2, it's important to find mentors who can help foster your growth and help prepare you for what will be required of you. But no matter what,

I think that you can always find a way to remain true to yourself and where you're from.

> As a Black woman, there are so many stereotypes that cast a shadow over me. I feel as if I constantly need to be careful about what I say, what I wear, or how I present myself in order to avoid being associated with those stereotypes and simultaneously avoid being labeled as unprofessional.
>
> —Second-year public PhD student

> I think we can stay true to who we are and where we come from, but it is so hard especially for people who don't have others around for support, reminding them that the world is so much bigger than grad school and yes it isn't built for those of us who are not White. And for me it has been very effortful; it's not a simple, natural way of being. I have to assess why I am making the choices I have made and spending time with the people I spend time with, and remind myself what makes me most excited about this work that led me down this ridiculous path of grad school.
>
> —Predoctoral intern, private PsyD student

> I limit how much I speak about diversity/inclusion given the lack of diversity/inclusion in my cohort. I act extra professional around professors given my minority background and the wish to not be discriminated against.
>
> —Second-year private PhD student

So the question of how much you can be you as a professional is an ongoing question. I suggest that you never try to be someone or something that you're not. If it feels that you're expending too much energy to keep up with a particular appearance or maintain a certain image, I'd argue that you can relax a little bit. If you're a funny person, be a funny professional. If you're outgoing and extroverted in your personal life, be that way as a professional. If you're a high-strung and neurotic person, be that way as a professional. If you're a totally chaotic and irresponsible person, you should probably get your act together. The things that you like about yourself will likely be the things that others like about you too; if you incorporate those aspects of your personality into your professional identity, you'll likely be OK, even if you need to turn down the volume on those things.

The personal/professional boundary also depends on how much of *you* you want others to know about. Some students work to keep their personal lives very distinct from their professional ones. They might not tell others that they're struggling or that they have family problems, or they might not introduce others to a partner. Other students allow for less distance between personal and professional or often mingle the two. Provided that you're acting ethically and not always complaining about something, there's no right or wrong answer to that equation, and your answer might change over time. Find your comfort zone, allow for that comfort zone to change, and find a place that works for you.

Owning It

In my third year of graduate school, I sat in a large conference room at the hospital where I had just started a practicum. Around the tables in the room were nurses, psychiatrists, my supervisor, occupational therapists, teachers, and administrators, most of whom I'd not yet met and many of whom had been working in the field since before I was born. It was morning rounds, when we reviewed the progress of all the patients in the hospital. Suddenly I heard the chief psychiatrist call my name: "Steve, do you think this girl is ready to be discharged?" *Wait, what?!* I thought. *I've only met with this kid a couple of times, I just started last week, my only previous clinical experience was a year of pretty cozy and well-supervised outpatient work in our training clinic, and I have no clue what I'm doing or how to even make that decision! How should I know?!* But then I remembered that the patient was stable, had been relatively good on the unit, and had a family who was eager to take her home. "Yeah," I replied, "good to go."

It can be unnerving to carry the title "psychologist in training." Other staff at your practicum sites may look to you for guidance or advice on treatment plans or diagnoses. It's sobering to come to grips with the effects your opinion can have while you're also realizing how much you have left to learn.

—Stephanie, fifth-year public PhD student

In my first year of grad school, I gave a presentation at a national conference. I stood in front of a room of seasoned professionals and rolled through a study that my advisor had given to me to do on some aspect of the MMPI-2. In the audience that day were some of the most accomplished MMPI-2 researchers in the world; my expertise on the MMPI-2 was limited to the five or six studies I'd read to get a general sense of what my study was about. Simply put, I had no idea what I was talking about in a room full of people who knew more than I could've imagined. And when I was asked a question, I fumbled through it as best I could; luckily everyone was kind.

It's daunting to think of myself as a professional. There is so much to learn, and I have to keep reminding myself that I will never know everything . . . despite being surrounded by professors that appear as if they know everything.

—Natassia, second-year private PhD student

These stories are only two of the times that I've had to step blindly into the role of a professional; there have been countless others. At a certain point in your training, you'll need to step into a professional role when you might not feel fully prepared. You might be in the company of others who know more than you do (or have a lot more experience), and you'll be doing your best impersonation of someone who knows what they're talking about. First session, first conference presentation, first class, first interaction with a psychologist you admire, dissertation defense, and so on—all of these events are fodder for some serious imposter syndrome, but that's OK, and it does get easier. And, just like becoming a clinician, at some point you'll be a professional psychologist without even recognizing the transition.

Picturing a Life

The personal growth you'll experience during your time in graduate school is likely to be remarkable. Some of that growth is just a function of the fact that we're talking about a five-year journey; lots of change happens in five years regardless. But, as I've mentioned, psychology graduate school often brings about a lot of self-exploration and reflection on personal factors, desires, and history. It can be exciting, but also painful and frustrating at times. And yet, in this shifting landscape of *youness*, you're supposed to figure out what you want to do with your life? Tall order.

Even if you don't have crystal clarity on the type of work you'd like to do, I expect that you can envision a particular lifestyle that will feel right for you. Are you a city person? How important is making lots of money? Do you want to own your own island? Do you want to be a well-known researcher? Do you want to live abroad? Do you want to work with the most vulnerable of populations? How important is job security versus flexibility? Is there a part of the country that you'd like to live in to help facilitate hobbies or interests? Do you have family obligations or connections that will dictate where and how you live? It will help you to consider the answers to these and other lifestyle questions as you navigate graduate school. Remember, graduate school is at least *partly* a means to an end, so it's important that the training goals you set for yourself are consistent with the lifestyle they'll afford you.

> My goal is to now have multiple streams of income after graduating. Given the amount of loans I will have to pay back, this is a necessity. Having seen this in practice with other psychologists since beginning grad school has made me more determined to achieve this.
>
> —Natassia, second-year private PhD student

Some important things to consider planning for are marriage and/or children. I've had students who had children before grad school, some who have had children during graduate school, and some who had children during internship. I've had students who have gotten married and some who have gotten divorced during graduate school too. You don't have to put your life on hold in order to be a graduate student, and having a life can often be a nice antidote to some of the sillier parts of the journey. Yet it does add some complications to the adventure.

Women graduate students, obviously, have more at stake in this question than do most of their male counterparts.[1] No matter how supportive a spouse, partner, or family may be, the burdens of pregnancy, poor sleep, breastfeeding, and so on are carried disproportionally by mothers. Although having kids as a graduate student can add some complications, it doesn't mean that you need to put off family to some unforeseen distant future. As is true for most things, however, timing is everything. I've observed that having a child in the year prior to internship or postdoc can be good options. During internship and postdoc, you're more likely to be working regular 9–5ish hours (provided that you're done with your dissertation), which facilitates day care and other supports available to working parents. No matter what, school and training settings will accommodate at least some family leave for new parents.

If you have a child or are planning on having one during graduate school, it seems that one of the most complicated things to figure out is your predoctoral internship application strategy. I mentioned this subject in Chapter 8, but too many geographical restrictions on your internship applications will reduce your chances of a successful match. However, I've seen many students figure out a workable solution to all of these problems, even if those solutions weren't necessarily ideal. Remember that you're a person first and a student second, so do what's going to make the most sense given what you want from your life, even if that choice introduces some complexity.

· · · · · · · · · · · · · · · · ·   **Tips and Strategies**   · · · · · · · · · · · · · · · ·

1. Act like a professional, even if you don't feel that way.
2. Observe professionalism in others. See what will work for you and what won't.
3. It's never too early to start life planning. Talk to older colleagues and professors about when and how they made decisions about marriage and having children.

· ·

In the three, four, five, or nine years that you're in graduate school, you'll undergo a transformation. You'll enter as a student but leave as a newly minted professional psychologist. That transformation is wonderful to witness, but it comes with its own share of growing pains. Part of the journey of graduate school is finding a way to navigate your personal growth, your professional growth, and the merging of the two. And remember that the professional you are now is not the professional that you will be. Be open to change, witness your own growth, and keep your eyes focused on what's most meaningful to you.

Reference

Neimeyer, G. J., Taylor, J. M., Rozensky, R. H., & Cox, D. R. (2014). The diminishing durability of knowledge in professional psychology: A second look at specializations. *Professional Psychology: Research and Practice*, 45(2), 92–98. http://dx.doi.org/10.1037/a0036176

[1] Except for same-sex male couples who adopt.

CHAPTER 10

Get a Life!

" I wish I just had time to think about the things I'm learning, but I can't. I'm so busy doing stuff that I can't stop to think about anything!" An advanced graduate student sat in my office with tears in her eyes, overwhelmed and exhausted. As an advisor, I realized that I'd neglected some aspects of her personhood. As a student, she realized that she hadn't let me know how bad things were getting. We worked together to offload as much work as feasible to give her a little more breathing room so that she could find her footing again. I've had a number of these conversations over the years. Sometimes things can get better; sometimes things just need to be endured. Either way, with all the pressures, time constraints, and emotional ups and downs, graduate school can really shove you off balance.

If you're like most graduate students, you're probably in your mid- to late 20s, single, and without children. Many of your friends from college are working jobs, starting families, and doing adult stuff. You'll spend a lot of time alone, reading and writing. It's a lonely road at times, and you might begin to feel a little out of step with other folks your age (other than your student colleagues). And this period of time in your life is one of rapid change, leading to (hopefully!) a growing sense of mastery and responsibility. With all of these pressures to change, to grow, to perform, and to learn, it's hard to remember to be a human being with time to actually *think*.

Taking Care of Yourself While You Take Care of Others

Being a therapist is hard. Being a student is hard. Being a human being is hard. Being all three of those things at once can sometimes be overwhelming. *Self-care* is one of those buzzwords that drives me a little crazy. I'm not sure that anyone really knows what it means (unless it's said ironically), and it seems that the lip service paid to the psychological needs of students and student therapists is pretty insufficient. Taking care of ourselves as we help others is an ethical mandate, and we need to work hard to carve out time and space to recharge ourselves.

Unlike other healing professions, as therapists, our only tools are ourselves and our words. When we're overwhelmed, limited, lost, or hurt, we usually can't be helpful to others. Given the difficulty of learning clinical work while also performing in the classroom, students are often pulled thin in terms of both time and emotional resources. Unfortunately, many graduate programs don't give students enough permission to take the breaks they need until things get really bad.

Self-care means doing something, anything, that even if just for a moment reminds me of my capabilities and my identity beyond being in academia.

—Second-year public PhD student

In a 2012 *New York Times* article titled "The 'Busy' Trap," writer Tim Kreider notes how being busy (or saying that you're busy) is a status symbol in our culture. Research has supported this idea such that when we (in America, at least) perceive someone as being really busy, we're more likely to see them as being of higher status. You hear it in the hallways: "How are you?" "BUSY!" Although we like to be busy, we don't generally like it all the time (and even if we do, we eventually crack). Psychology graduate students (and their obnoxious professors) are generally no different. Saying that you're busy is a sign of importance, of status, and of dedication (it is also a way of telling others to leave you alone). We say this even when we know that time for relationships, exercise, and sleep are essential components of mental health. Wouldn't it be nice if our culture saw *balance* as a more prized goal? "How are you?" "BALANCED!"

From what I've seen, students tend to get mixed messages about self-care. On one hand, a program might espouse an ideal of self-care, but should a student actually confess that they're taking a break or that they're unavailable to do an additional research project because they're spending time with family, they're often met with either covert or overt derision. I've also heard faculty comment behind closed doors things like "I didn't take care of myself in grad school, so I'm not sure why they need to. Grad school is supposed to suck." Even if students don't get immediate negative feedback for self-care, it can create the impression in some faculty members' minds that the student lacks commitment or isn't a team player. Furthermore, even if a program encourages self-care, a student might still struggle with whether it's *really* OK to have balance. Again, all of this strikes me as ironic given that these are *psychology* graduate programs!

Missing out on opportunities is a negative consequence of self-care. It's always good to remember that those opportunities will come around again, though.

—Second-year private PhD student

Of course, this does not describe *all* psychology programs or *any* psychology programs *all of the time*. Some programs will be more forgiving and care oriented than others. And even the most time-intensive program will have ebbs and dips in intensity. In those times when things are easier, you might find yourself with ample free time to pursue relationships, solo time, and personal growth. If you find yourself in one of those programs or in a downtime phase, rejoice and enjoy it (without guilt). Practicing self-care now will pay off in the future.

Balancing the role of student and therapist is no easy task. Add on TA responsibilities, research, classes, emails, life outside of school and work (what's that?), relationships, eating healthy food and exercising, and family stuff . . . whew! Just listing it all makes me overwhelmed. It is not easy to balance this 25-hour-per-day lifestyle, but I remind myself that it is temporary, and that gets me through it. At the same time, I also make time for myself and try not to feel guilty watching TV or reading a book for fun. I also play in a band, and that helps ground me a bit outside of the school and work world. In addition, I started going to therapy, which has not only helped me with different life situations but also helped me become a way better therapist.

—Josh, fourth-year public PhD student

I can promise you that there will be low points during your graduate school career. Those low points might not be the lowest points in your life, but dips are inevitable. Academic failures, clinical stresses, relationships with your advisor and/or peers, breakups, financial challenges, family problems, or regrets about getting a dog (see Chapter 1) might increase your stress beyond the tipping point. Ideally, you'll have a great therapist who can help you identify when you're running into trouble (see Chapter 11), but I'd urge you to make self-care more of a lifestyle choice than merely a response to feeling overwhelmed.

Nobody taught me what self-care means as a therapist. So it is stressful when there are big clinical moments that impact me and I don't know how to process that. Some supervisors are awesome at talking through this, but some are not. Knowing how to care for myself after caring for my patients is important so I don't burn out, but it can be hard to know what to do after it.

—Third-year private PsyD student

Consider those activities that you can do each day that make you feel like an even better version of yourself. Have a standing dinner appointment with a friend, have a gym routine, eat lunch outside, run, meditate, go to church, paint, go to the movies, cook good food, or (gasp!) read a book for pleasure. Set goals for yourself that have nothing to do with schoolwork (e.g., a fitness regimen, learning to play an instrument, taking foreign language classes, watching every James Bond movie). Expand your horizons and learn new things that will bring you joy for years to come. Little things, practiced daily, can give you time, space, and energy to follow through on the rest of your life. As a student once said to me, "Learning how to half-ass schoolwork to spend a little more time with my family has been one of the best lessons of grad school." Regardless of what things you do to take care of yourself, make a commitment to them and try to absolve yourself of any guilt that goes with not doing schoolwork at every waking moment. In the end, self-care is an investment in your education.

To take care of myself, I stay intellectually curious, maintain a good sense of humor, save time for friends and family, and always try to get a good night of sleep.

—Fourth-year private PsyD student

Something that has helped me manage the stress of providing clinical services has been the personal adage of "Do the best you can with what you got." Specifically, this has helped me to cope with the stress created by trying to balance the drive to feel useful to clients right away while also encountering the many real barriers to therapeutic growth outside a clinician's locus of control.

—Ari, fourth-year public PhD student

The most important lesson I've taken away from a particularly difficult personal year amidst my graduate school training is to maintain passion in my own life. I would advise any student to make sure they participate in activities that provide them with a feeling of joy and engagement. For me, reengaging in salsa dancing was more effective than any talk therapy I've ever been in. These types of hobbies will help maintain a strong emotional immune system so that when particularly stressful periods of graduate school arise, you are best equipped to face them. Even finding little moments to savor in times of stress can provide immense relief. Treat yourself to a good meal, watch funny shows on Netflix, dance, explore nature, have mini-adventures, and laugh with friends. Through it all, ignore the voice saying, *You should be doing work right now*. I found that as tired as I was, when I made the effort to go dancing, I noticed a positive shift in my mood the next day.

—Third-year private PsyD student

· · · · · · · · · · · · · · · · · **Words of Wisdom** · · · · · · · · · · · · · · · · · · ·

1. Enjoy the downtimes and lulls in action without guilt or anxiety.
2. Make time for love, friends, and family. Supportive and loving people help us maintain balance.
3. Ask for help and support from a faculty member you trust. If you're struggling, don't do so in silence. Others are available to help and will be happy to do so.

Love

Freud famously once said that the two most important things are love and work. As a graduate student, you've got the *work* part pretty well dialed in. In fact, you've probably excelled at work for a really long time. Because you're all set with work, let's talk about love. It turns out that your heart needs as much attention as your mind. Don't neglect your heart. If you neglect your heart long enough, you'll end up as a lonely grump. Work *and* love.

Dating as a graduate student can be a challenge, particularly in a smaller town where everyone knows each other and your students or therapy clients can see your profile on Tinder (or whatever you kids are up to these days). And no matter what, when you tell people you're a psychology graduate student, you'll need to endure a litany of questions like "Are you analyzing me right now?"[1] (which should probably be a deal breaker). However, the biggest challenge is likely the difficulty with time. Free time is a scarce commodity when you're balancing academics, research, and clinical practice. Finding time to date or foster new relationships can be a challenge. Even if you have the time to date, you might not take it because it's nice to have an evening off every now and again. In my experience, the students who make dating work in graduate school are of two kinds: (a) students who have a real commitment to finding a relationship or (b) students who enjoy dating for the sake of dating and are not looking for a relationship. In the middle ground between wanting and not wanting a relationship is the stress of ambivalence.

Another difficulty in grad school dating is the one presented by the internship year. It's likely that you'll need to move away to complete your internship year, which can be a real barrier if your partner is not portable. Navigating the internship match and geographic preferences/restrictions can be a real challenge. Some students choose to spend a year (or two) apart, but others choose to limit their applications to a narrow geographic area, and others have a partner who is able to make a career sacrifice. No matter what, internship application time is often a period of significant relationship complexity.

Finally, our work is emotionally draining. The stress of class work is one thing, but maintaining a caseload of clients can really tap you out. Seeking the emotional wherewithal at the end of a long day to talk about some relationship process might make you want to rip your hair out. Like all good things, relationships can also be stressful, and there will be times when your heart doesn't need more stress. Of course, your partner might be your very best source of support in those really hard times.

If the person doesn't understand the commitment and isn't supportive, then it's pointless to try to start something.

—Fourth-year public PhD student

---

[1] Get used to this question—people will ask it for the rest of your career. When I get the question these days, I simply say "yes" and then stare blankly. Many students circumvent the question by lying or being vague. When I was a student, I told conversant strangers that I was in dentistry school. No one wants to talk about their teeth when they're seated next to you on an airplane.

Being in graduate school definitely makes starting romantic relationships more difficult. There is rarely time to date, and if you do have a date, you are often stressed about something and potentially not fun to be around. It can also be hard for people outside of the field to relate to. It is also difficult to date when on a graduate student budget.

— Third-year private PhD student

I have very little time to get to know someone. In between classes, research, seeing clients, and managing my own mental health, I don't have time to date. I don't have time for small talk! I have a paper to publish! I don't have time for coffee! I'm drinking it as I walk to class!

— Second-year public PhD student

Of course, some of you will come to graduate school with a relationship intact. Some will be married, engaged, or well settled in a long-term committed partnership. Those loving relationships will need extra maintenance as well because of the same challenges of time, focus, and intensity. The other thing that makes relationship maintenance a challenge is how much changing you'll be doing. Four or five years pack a lot of change regardless, but going through graduate school forces a lot of self-reflection and growth that might take your partner by surprise. It's important to be open about those changes and do the work needed to help the relationship survive (or not).

There is so much change happening within myself (especially given the particular field I'm in) that it can be emotional, and that makes it hard to want to enter into a romantic relationship that will warrant its own strong emotions as well.

— Second-year private PhD student

No matter the relationship, either brand new or well established, love in graduate school is important. It's food for your heart, and the support of a loving partner during the challenging parts of grad school can be a lifesaver. Focus on a relationship can also provide a feeling of balance, a connection with a larger community, and it will keep you from feeling that your entire life is on hold. There are challenges, yes, but those challenges can be navigated, and the benefit is well worth it.

I met my husband two months before I started my PhD program, and we got married right after I finished my third year. Being a married grad student is difficult at times because I don't get to be the wife that I'd like to be at times. For example, I can't always take time to spend time with my husband in the evening or on weekends. He learned quickly to keep himself busy and make friends in a new place. Other significant others in the program become great friends because they "get it." My husband is extremely supportive, and so I haven't had to limit myself in terms of internship locations or opportunities. I have had peers with significant others that are less supportive, and it makes it extremely difficult. My husband is very good about not making me feel guilty when I "fail" as a wife some weeks—like forgetting to do the one thing he asked me to do that week because I had a lot on my mind or getting home late (again) because of a client crisis. He also does at least half or more of the household chores, cooking, and taking care of our dog since his job allows him to be home more than me. His support makes all the difference.

—Fourth-year public PhD student

Your Wacko Family

If you're like me (and everyone else), you have a wacko family. In fact, your wacko family is probably one of the main reasons that you're in this field. As you embark on the graduate school journey, you might find that your relationships with your family members will change a little bit. Granted, it's likely that many of you have served as pseudotherapists for your family for as long as you can remember, but that might get worse as soon as you register for your very first graduate class. As a student once said to me, "I was about five minutes into my first quarter when my mom lost the last of her boundaries with me." Welcome to the profession.

I have less time for family, but they are very understanding about that.

—Natassia, second-year private PhD student

Managing those family boundaries can be a challenge. As is true for some friends, you might find yourself feeling a bit used by some family members who want some free and wildly unethical therapy. Your desire to help and feel useful might end up becoming a big hurdle in setting boundaries as well. Setting those boundaries is important. In those times when I've felt somewhat *used*, I've never been let down by saying to a friend or family member, "Gosh, that sounds rough. Do you have a therapist?" That usually does the trick.

Of course, most people in your wacko family will be really supportive and helpful in your time in graduate school. If they've not been to graduate school themselves, they might not understand what you're doing fully, but it's likely they'll be proud and offer an ear of support when needed. As is true for romantic love, make time for your family. For international students, it might be hard to visit your family often, but a brief video chat could really brighten your day. If nothing else, you need your family to cheer for you when you get your diploma.

If you're the first in your family to go to college or graduate school, your time in grad school might also end up making you feel a little (or a lot) different from your family. If you're entering new educational territory for your family, there will be a time when you can no longer explain to them what it is you're doing. I was still an undergrad when I just started to tell my mom I was busy doing "psychology stuff"; even after I got my PhD, she still would refer to me as a psychiatrist from time to time. For many of you, the process of graduate school will also entail a somewhat painful (or at least disconcerting) feeling of separation from your family of origin. As you get acculturated into the field of psychology, your family culture might feel a little less comfortable than it did before. You might end up feeling relatively bicultural such that you still have the values and experiences of home but you've also hung out in an ivory tower or two. I've heard many students' stories of having to navigate that difference and find ways to remain comfortable with their families when they have chosen a life path that is so different.

Being Out of Balance

I think there's a dotted line separating the feelings of being *overwhelmed*, *impaired*, and *burned out*. Certainly, these are related concepts that all have to do with not having enough personal resources left to handle the stresses of our job (both clinical and academic). And just because you might be dealing with some life stressor doesn't mean that you're at all impaired. Indeed, I was speaking with a graduate student the other day who had recently gone through a prolonged breakup; instead of impaired as a clinician, she found that she felt most like herself during sessions and that her work as a therapist was a brief refuge from the temporary complexities of her own life. She clearly had the emotional wherewithal to compartmentalize well, and my guess is that many of you could do so too.

Sometimes it might be useful to let someone else know that you're struggling. Your advisor, DCT, department chair, or clinical supervisor are often good choices. When I was a predoctoral intern, I was going through a nasty breakup with someone I'd been with for eight years. I asked all of my supervisors to keep an eye on me. I reasoned that I felt OK but I might not be able to notice that I was slipping, not being fully attentive, or that my clinical reasoning might be impaired. By inviting my supervisors into my vigilance, I knew that I had allies, was acting ethically, and had forced myself into some degree of accountability.

Mental health challenges among psychology graduate students are another one of those "ironic" situations where graduate school can be somewhat unforgiving. Those of you who suffer from (or have suffered from) depression, anxiety, substance abuse, and other such conditions might find that your graduate program is not always sensitive to your needs. There's no reason that emotional struggles should prevent you from successfully completing your graduate program, but it might mean that you need a little more time. You'll need to be the judge of how much of your mental health needs you'll share with faculty and colleagues, but I suggest that you reach out to the office that helps students with disabilities. If you can avail yourself of extended time, flexible scheduling, or the like to help your progression through school, go for it.

Being a grad student with mental health challenges is the F-ing worst. I didn't realize how much of a difference it would make. I felt like I was working twice as hard as my peers, but half as productive. It takes time to stay emotionally balanced. I also didn't realize how stigmatizing it would be to have depression and anxiety in a clinical psychology program. It did make me question my ability to be an effective clinician. It turns out, in some ways, it helped me become a better clinician—I more deeply understand and connect with the pain my patients have experienced. That also meant I had to really take care of myself when I was working with patients. I had a psychiatrist and a psychologist, but I also needed support within my program. I was lucky to have a supervisor who valued authenticity and was open to discussing challenges I experienced both as a grad student in general and as a clinician. His validation and acceptance of me as a whole person helped me feel less alone during my grad school journey.

—Predoctoral intern, public PhD student

It's unlikely that you'll experience clinical burnout during your time in graduate school, likely because you won't have been at the job long enough. It's normal to need a break, but feeling really burned out is a different matter entirely. If you are feeling burned out on clinical work in a short period of time, it might be that your cases are too complex for your current level of training. But you might find yourself burned out on school and obnoxious professors. Academic burnout (i.e., "senioritis") is probably not as serious as clinical burnout because the only one who suffers is you (and some of your obnoxious professors). If you find yourself running a bit thin on resources, speak up and ask for help. Little problems can quickly turn into big ones if you ignore them. In many programs, students often feel compelled to appear as though they have it all together, but don't let impression management get in the way of doing what's right for you and your clients.

· · · · · · · · · · · · · · · · · **Tips and Strategies** · · · · · · · · · · · · · · · · ·

1. Seek ways to expand yourself beyond school requirements. Hobbies and goals that are outside of psychology will remind you that you're not just a student.
2. Get used to the question "Are you psychoanalyzing me?" because you'll hear it for the rest of your life.
3. Nurture your relationships, both new and old. They'll be there for you in your hardest and best moments.

· ·

Taking care of ourselves should not be an antidote to real life; it should be the way we all seek to live all the time. As a student, your job is stressful, and finding ways to offload some of that stress and invest in your mental and physical health will serve dividends for the rest of your life. Avoid the busy trap, find love, and give your mom a call. You'll be glad you did.

Seriously. Put down this book and go do something interesting. Right now.

CHAPTER 11

Sitting in the Other Chair
Personal Therapy

As a graduate student, I resisted therapy for myself for a long time. In my mind, I figured that I'd go if things got really bad or if I was struggling with some form of severe diagnosable condition. But finally, in the summer after my third year, I decided to give it a whirl. The decisions and events that got me there are complex, but I recall that I had a client who was clearly capable of greater insight and reflection than I was. He could go places in our work that I couldn't follow because I lacked the self-awareness to meet him where he was. It was a wildly disconcerting process that finally showed me how blind to myself I really was.

My first therapist was a Jungian psychiatrist (yeah, that's right . . . a Jungian psychiatrist). He greeted me while wearing shorts, a T-shirt, and hiking boots. His office was a jumble of books about dreams and fairy tales along with a well-worn copy of the *Physician's Desk Reference*. He fiddled with river stones while we talked, and he told stories about himself that helped me consider myself in different ways. In short, he was exactly the opposite of everything that I'd ever thought about what a therapist should be.

It was great. In that first session, I was hooked. In our meetings, I felt seen, understood, and cared for. He gave me a great education on how to be oneself as a therapist in a way that felt really freeing for me as a therapist in training. My work as a therapist improved (or at least changed) dramatically as I adopted some of his mannerisms and catchphrases (many of which I still use).[1] More important, I learned about me in a way that allowed me to have greater, deeper, and more personal connections with the clients I see (as well as the loved ones in my life).

Since that time, I've had two more therapists. The most significant work I've done was a multiyear psychoanalysis (five days a week on the couch!) that brought about more changes than I can possibly describe. Despite some initial hesitation when I was a grad student, I now think of personal therapy as one of the most important experiences of my life. I'm not sure where I'd be as a therapist, academic, husband, or father without it.

---

[1] Two of my favorites: He always ended our sessions by kindly and politely saying, "Steve, go away." When negotiating his fees, he said, "Let's find a fee that hurts both of us to the same degree."

125

It turns out that I'm not alone. Norcross (2005) notes that most (about 75 percent) mental health workers will have their own psychotherapy, and more than 50 percent will have more than one discrete course of therapy. As is true for all clients, psychologists who have personal therapy report improvements in personal well-being and relationships with others. At this point, research does not support the idea that therapy makes for better therapists, but there is some literature to suggest that it improves therapists' alliance with their clients (Gold & Hilsenroth, 2009). No matter what the true impact of therapy on their work, psychologists are clear that personal psychotherapy is an important part of their training and professional development (see Norcross, 2005, for a review).

Do it! I don't think you will regret it. It has made graduate school much more bearable, and it has taught me a lot about therapy.

—Josh, fourth-year public PhD student

· · · · · · · · · · · · · · · · · · **Words of Wisdom** · · · · · · · · · · · · · · · ·

1. Psychotherapy is an investment in your life, relationships, and work.
2. Personal therapy teaches you what psychotherapy is really like.
3. Psychotherapy helps you see a professional clinical life for yourself.

· ·

Professional Development

Several psychology graduate programs require personal therapy for their students. Other programs are really encouraging of therapy, and discussion of personal therapy fits neatly in the culture of the program. Of course, many other programs might make information and resources available, but it's still not spoken about, or perhaps there's even stigma. These cultural differences are important and might make it more or less likely for a student to seek personal therapy.

Our program does not require personal therapy. They give lip service to it being important, but the program has a culture that rewards looking like you have everything together. So nobody talks about being in therapy. That culture makes being in therapy even more important!

—Nicole, third-year private PsyD student

I am really frustrated and disappointed that my program does not provide free psychotherapy. I feel that this is something that should be prioritized.

—Third-year private PsyD student

Norcross's research suggests that personal therapy is ranked as one of the most important formative events in psychotherapists' training, even above didactics and course work. One reason for this is pretty clear: It's one of the only ways in training that you can see an entire course of therapy conducted by an experienced therapist. You can watch all the APA videos you like, but those are only a few sessions and not weeks and weeks of ups and downs. Unless you get the opportunity to be a cotherapist with a supervisor, the likelihood that you'll see a whole treatment outside of your own is close to zero.

My program does not require personal therapy, but it is encouraged by my advisor and peers. I do not feel any stigma around the topic among peers and faculty, but it would be nice if the program helped pay for it or was more involved and invested in students' mental health.

—Josh, fourth-year public PhD student

Not only can you see a therapist apply their trade, but you actually get to *feel* the results on a moment-by-moment basis. You'll get to see what feels good, what doesn't land, what is helpful and clarifying, and what just confuses you. Apart from reading about the importance of the therapeutic alliance, you'll actually feel how important it is from the other chair. You'll likely experience an increase in empathy for your clients and a greater sense of patience for yourself as a clinician, and you'll learn to trust the therapeutic process. Nothing teaches us more than direct experience, and therapy is no different.

I find myself using a lot of the same phrases, techniques, boundary setting, and styles as my therapist with my own clients. It has definitely affected the way I do therapy.

—Fourth-year public PhD student

The other professional development piece is simple *modeling*. In the same way that I felt freed by seeing a therapist who was relaxed and comfortable in a T-shirt and shorts, you can see how a therapist greets you, discusses fees, ends a therapy hour, arranges their office, deals with confidentiality, and generally comports themselves as professionals. You'll learn more therapeutic catchphrases than you can imagine (on a weekly basis, I borrow memorable quotes from all three of my therapists). As you learn their style and observe how they interact with you, you can begin to see what might work for you as a professional and what might not. Will you have personal photos around? Do you want to have a home office or set up shop in an office building? Will you refer to yourself as Dr. So-and-So or go by your first name? How will you dress? How will you deal with personal disclosure? How will you start and end sessions? All of these questions come up for therapists in training, and the modeling of a real-life therapist helps you begin to see your clinical career in greater relief. It's cool like that.

While many of my colleagues articulated a lot of anxiety at first seeing clients, I didn't find this to be the case for me. I think this had a lot to do with having done many courses of therapy in different orientations. While I didn't know exactly what to do or say as a beginning clinician, the therapy process didn't seem shrouded in secrecy because I had experienced it as a client.

—Third-year private PsyD student

I feel more confident in employing techniques or approaches as a clinician that I have personal experience with as a client.

—Ari, fourth-year public PhD student

But the Real Work Is Personal

Although personal therapy is great professional development, the biggest gains are for you personally. Of course, if we're doing well personally, it's likely that we'll also function better professionally, but even apart from the downstream benefits to our clinical and academic work, the primary benefit of therapy for you is personal. Unless you're a weirdo hermit, you have friends and relationships, and we've already established that you have a wacko family. Personal therapy for you is likely to improve or change those relationships to be more genuine, caring, and real. In short, therapy is important for you for the same reasons it's important for anyone: to improve your capacity to engage in more rewarding relationships with yourself and those around you. Citing Norcross (2005) again, most therapists choose psychodynamic, humanistic, or eclectic therapists for their own work, suggesting that most therapists are not there for simple symptom reduction or behavior change. It's about relationships!

Therapy has allowed me to accept that I am doing my best and that this is good enough. I often feel guilty if I don't give a lot of effort to class assignments, research, papers, etc., but sometimes I just do not have the time to do everything with 100 percent effort. It's been hard, but I've learned to not put so much weight on stuff like that.

—Josh, fourth-year public PhD student

In addition to the relational component of the work, graduate school is stressful and is likely to beat you up a bit. Learning how to do therapy is even more stressful than academic stuff, and it will challenge you in a very different way. Personal therapy gives you a place to go with that stress to decompress, vent, and gain perspective. Talk about the stress of school, challenges with clients and supervisors, and the icky stuff you've learned about yourself since starting the graduate school journey. If you're a psychology graduate student and you see a psychologist for therapy, they've been right where you are, struggled with some of the same issues, and dealt with the same nonsense academic red tape. It's hard to find that type of empathy from anyone else! Finding a place to park some of that stress will free you up to have a new perspective and a lightened load when you head back to the psychology building.

I have had a few courses of therapy with different orientations. My most recent therapist is the DCT of a counseling program I elected not to attend. I respected his intelligence and depth of knowledge (and knowledge about psychology graduate school).

—Third-year private PsyD student

Personal therapy has been a bedrock of my ability to survive graduate school. It is not normal what we do to ourselves in these programs. As such, it is incredibly beneficial to have an ally who has come through the other end and understands the process.

—Ari, fourth-year public PhD student

Of course, as we discussed in Chapter 10, many students struggle with mental health challenges during their time in grad school that are beyond simple stress or angst. If you're one of the many students who struggle with issues such as depression and anxiety, you're not alone. Recent research suggests that about a third of students experience depression and/or anxiety while in psychology graduate school (Rummell, 2015). Dealing with challenges that are more complex than mere stress makes personal therapy a near necessity. If that's the case for you, it's important to be proactive about getting connected with a therapist (and maybe a psychiatrist) as soon as you begin school. Getting ahead of challenging times will save you some pain down the road.

Sometimes we need to sacrifice our own needs to keep up with our class work or caseloads, but it is important to continually check in with your internal world. Know the warning signs of falling back into dangerous emotional territory, and know when it is time to reach out for help. As psychologists in training, we are often the worst clients, but find a good therapist to establish a relationship with. Let yourself be a patient instead of the practitioner. The multiple roles of being in a clinical psychology program all require immense emotional energy. I've learned that it is easy to let being a student and a therapist deprive your friends, partners, and family members of the best version of yourself.

—Third-year private PsyD student

The Personal and the Professional

In my mind, a therapist without insight is like a surgeon with just one hand. Sure, they can probably do the job, but it might be a little more difficult for everyone involved. In addition to the personal benefits of dealing with relationships and graduate school stress, therapy gives you greater personal insight into who you are, what you've been through, and what activates you, frightens you, and freaks you out. As therapists, our only tools are our reactions, our knowledge, and our words. And it's important that those words usually come from a place of caring and service to the patient rather than from fear, avoidance, or countertransference on our part. As we have greater clarity about our own internal landscape, we can have greater clarity about our responses to our clients. Greater clarity then leads to greater wisdom in how to best respond to those who come to us for help. True, research has not shown that personal therapy increases therapist effectiveness, but therapists who have experienced therapy do report greater feelings of connection with their clients. Therapy seems like a solid investment in our work as therapists and in the relationships we have with our loved ones.

Personal therapy has been invaluable! It helps me process the many stressors of learning to be a clinician while also letting me better understand my best tool as a clinician: myself.

—Nicole, third-year private PsyD student

I believe that a strong foundation of insight into one's self is fundamental to my work as a clinician. As such, my experiences in personal therapy help to strengthen this base with each session.

—Ari, fourth-year public PhD student

Pragmatics

If you're planning on going to therapy, you need to track down a therapist, arm wrestle them to give you a break on fees (or take your insurance), and then make sure that they don't end up being your next supervisor. So, how do you find a therapist? You could Google "cheap therapist who will help me with my clown phobia," but I think you can be a bit more systematic than that.

The first question you'll need to answer is whether you plan on using your insurance. It's an unfortunate fact that many therapists don't take health insurance (the ratio of paperwork to payment is woefully terrible for most plans), but if you have student health insurance and you live in a university town, you'll probably be in luck (e.g., the only insurance I take in my private practice is the student health insurance). Your insurance company can provide you with a list of practitioners who take your insurance and who are accepting new patients.

Of course, that list can be really, really long; a list of 100+ practitioners isn't helpful for finding a therapist. Once you have that list of therapists, you can take it to faculty in your department who might know who to recommend. If your faculty are disconnected from the local therapist scene (as is often the case), many locations have regional psychological associations with searchable websites. I encourage students to take the list of insurance-approved therapists and cross-check with a searchable database of local psychologists to narrow the list down. It all takes some work.

My advice to new graduate students about personal psychotherapy is simple— DO IT! Not only is it incredibly helpful for your own survival in the program, but it is also a valuable opportunity to further your own development as a clinician.

—Fourth-year public PhD student

Often the best way to find a therapist is merely to ask other students about whom they see. Your department might also maintain a list of psychologists in town who will adjust their fees for broke graduate students. No matter what, it's acceptable (and even encouraged) to shop around. You test-drive multiple cars before you pick one you like; entrusting your mental health to someone should be no different. Just be clear up front that you're meeting with a few different therapists to find the right fit, and I'm sure that everyone will be accommodating. Also be clear up front that you'll need a fee adjustment so they can tell you if it's even worth having an initial meeting.

I found my therapist through a referral from the university health center. I first met with a social worker there who then referred me to my current therapist in the community.

—Ari, fourth-year public PhD student

I contacted a psychoanalysis school to see if they had any students in need of cases. It was a low-cost way to find a therapist.

—Nicole, third-year private PsyD student

I found my therapist on PsychologyToday.com. She's great. I sent her an email and booked my first session about a year ago now.

—Josh, fourth-year public PhD student

One somewhat awkward thing about personal therapy is that you and your therapist might end up moving in somewhat similar professional circles. I think that it's useful for students to get involved with a local psychological association or other professional organizations for trainings and seminars and to stay abreast of legal issues that impact the profession. Of course, you might also bump into your therapist at some of those functions, which might make hanging out at the fruit plate and cheese platter a little weird. It's good to anticipate these things up front and have a discussion about how you would like your therapist to handle it. A therapist colleague once told me about a time when he was at a professional meeting where he was "introduced" to his graduate student client by another colleague. Weird, right? But not entirely unexpected.

Another challenge that students sometimes face is finding a therapist who shares their racial or ethnic background or who understands sexual diversity. This might be even more of an issue in smaller towns that lack diversity among practitioners. If that's the case for you and you feel most comfortable with someone of a similar background, the local psychological association is the place to start. If that search yields nothing, then consider finding a therapist out of the area who is willing to conduct video therapy. You can search professional organizations at the state or national level for referrals, or you can send a note to the local organization to see whether any of their members might have referrals.

One of the biggest barriers to personal therapy is the price. Many students have difficulty affording even a reduced fee (or even just a copay). Hopefully, you can find someone who will offer you a fee that you can afford, even if it means that you need to stretch a bit. One of my former supervisors once said that "mental health is worth a car payment," meaning that psychotherapy should be a priority in your spending (and should be worth at least what you'd be willing to pay for a car).

Think of it as an educational cost. It is a necessary part of becoming a balanced clinician.

—Nicole, third-year private PsyD student

The other thing to remember is that you can consider psychotherapy as a training expense. For that reason, it's tax deductible (provided you make enough money for itemized deductions). I've also heard of students using student loan money to pay for therapy, given that it's a central piece of their training toward the profession. None of these things totally remove the sting of paying for therapy, but they do make the sting hurt a little less.

I completely understand what it's like to be really, really broke. There were times in my training when I was living on credit cards and skipping meals to save cash. In that context, there's no way that I could afford therapy, even if it was just a few bucks a week as a copay. If you're in that situation, you probably have fewer options for personal psychotherapy, unfortunately. If you're at a university, you can take advantage of the services of the counseling center, which will likely give you a handful of sessions for free (which is better than nothing).[2]

---

[2] Of course, if you're likely to be placed in a practicum there at some point in your training, that might not be a very good choice for you.

There also might some free meet-up or support groups in town that you might take advantage of. Also, there are often low-cost clinics subsidized by charitable organizations or state or local governments where you might be able to be seen for free or for very little money. These options are likely to be very time limited and might require evidence of a diagnosable condition. If your finances prevent personal psychotherapy while you're in graduate school, it should be a priority as soon as you start pulling in the big-time predoc/postdoc dollars (which are only big time compared to being a grad student).

· · · · · · · · · · · · · · · · · **Tips and Strategies** · · · · · · · · · · · · · · ·

1. Find potential therapists from the online list provided by your local psychological association or lists maintained by your department, or ask older students whom they'd recommend.
2. Personal psychotherapy is a tax write-off and an educational expense that could be covered by student loans.
3. You can take potential therapists for test drives. Be clear about what you're looking for.

· ·

Psychotherapy for yourself is a gift that borders on a necessity. Clearly, it's common practice among those in the mental health field, and the benefits to your relationships, clients, and stress level are worth the hassle and the cost. If you can find a way to make the investment, you'll benefit in ways that you can't imagine. If nothing else, you'll see your future as a therapist with greater clarity than you otherwise might.

References

Gold, S. H., & Hilsenroth, M. J. (2009). Effects of graduate clinicians' personal therapy on therapeutic alliance. *Journal of Clinical Psychology and Psychotherapy, 16,* 159–171.

Norcross, J. C. (2005). The psychotherapist's own psychotherapy: Educating and developing psychologists. *American Psychologist, 60,* 840–850.

Rummell, C. M. (2015). An exploratory study of psychology graduate student workload, health, and program satisfaction. *Professional Psychology: Research and Practice, 46,* 391–399.

CHAPTER 12

So Why Bother?

Remembering the Big Picture

Thus far, we've concerned ourselves with some of the minutiae of what graduate school is like, the milestones that you'll need to complete, and the stresses of living a somewhat monastic lifestyle. Certainly, there are lot of details and little stresses along the way. But it's easy to get lost among the trees if you forget the layout of the forest. My hope is that we can spend this last chapter zooming back and outward into the larger picture of life, the universe, and everything.[1] In the process of zooming back, I hope that you can find the passion and desire that is propelling you toward this degree. I like to say that passion is like a lighthouse; it will always keep you pointed in the right direction when the seas get turbulent. Losing sight of that passion will make things so much more difficult than they need to be.

Sometimes, when things get hairy in my life, I go outside and look up at the stars. I think about how old the light is that's hitting my eyes and how ancient the universe is compared to human life on Earth. I imagine what our planet looks like to those stars and how small and insignificant it all is. I remember that our time here is limited and that all of human history is merely a blip in the expansiveness of time. Suddenly, in those moments of reflection, disagreements in faculty meetings seem a lot less meaningful than they did, and I give myself a bit of a break on the fact that I'm running behind schedule on a book I'm writing about navigating psychology graduate school. We need those moments of reflection when we can pull back and see the really, really *big* picture.

It may sound hokey, but the next time you're stressed over your qualifying exams, a test grade, or an interaction with a colleague, go outside and look at the stars (if you live in a big city, you might need to travel a bit) or whatever it is that helps you feel grounded. Think about the length of your life and how even your time in graduate school will be a distant and fuzzy memory. To be clear, seeing the big picture doesn't mean that the things you're dealing with are unimportant. Seeing the big picture merely helps you clarify what things *are* important and what's important about them. It's a nice reminder that what we can control is really, really small.

[1] 42, with all due respect to *The Hitchhiker's Guide to the Galaxy*.

So what does this wacky stargazing talk have to do with psychology graduate school, really? It's about passion. Remembering the reasons why you're in graduate school will help you through the lowest points and push you when you feel like giving up. Having a clear view of what's important and what your passions are will shield you against too much disappointment and personalization of setback. Acting in service of your passions will bring a joy to the work and a uniqueness to your experience that is priceless.

Finding Your Lighthouse

One of the things I love about acceptance and commitment therapy (ACT) (Hayes, Strosahl, & Wilson, 2011) is the focus on values. If we find what we truly value and live our lives according to those values, we won't get sidetracked by painful thoughts or feelings. The same is true for your graduate school journey. Your passions and your values compelled you toward this goofy field (where you'll be woefully underpaid compared to your friends who got computer science degrees) and will keep you moving when you need a push.

During a period of deep suffering in early adulthood, I seemingly discovered my own mind. With this, I began to see through the masks we all wear, and notice all the suffering around me. Working through my own suffering and witnessing the usefulness of introspective work gave me faith in the human capacity for healing and transformation, and motivated me to help people find meaning that makes life worth living, even in the face of suffering.

—Peter, fourth-year private PsyD student

To be honest, I don't think I had great reasons for going to graduate school for psychology. It seemed like the natural next step in my education, and not going would have felt like failure. Luckily, I'm still glad I went.

—Lauren, predoctoral intern, public PhD student

So, take a minute and reflect. Why did you (or will you) pursue graduate school in psychology? What are the good and altruistic reasons? What are the not-so-good reasons? What are the reasons that have to do with you, and what are the reasons that have to do with others? I urge you to even write those down and revisit them from time to time. As you continue to grow and learn more, those reasons might change, and that's OK as long as you don't lose sight of what makes this field right for you.

I wanted to go to graduate school in psychology because I wanted to make a difference in people's lives and I thought this was the perfect avenue for me to pursue that dream. I liked that I had the option to go into teaching at the university level or I could do private practice, or even both.

—Second-year public PhD student

I often felt drawn to professions with healing and meaning. On a practical level, it felt impossible to use liberal arts degrees without higher education. I also just really like people. I loved the idea of working with people in such an honest and vulnerable way.

—Natalie, third-year private PsyD student

I came to graduate school because of my passion for research in psychology and my interest in understanding how to help students thrive in home and school environments.

—Third-year public PhD student

I came to graduate school for flexibility in career options, financial opportunities, and financial stability.

—Third-year public PhD student

I was motivated to go to graduate school by my desire to have career options down the line. I knew I wanted to work with people in a helping profession. Beyond that, I didn't know what I wanted to do. I believed that going to graduate school would help me focus my interests and that earning a PhD would open a lot of doors. And if we're being honest, part of me wanted to avoid joining the "real world" for as long as possible.

—Lindsey, predoctoral intern, public PhD student

· · · · · · · · · · · · · · · · · **Words of Wisdom** · · · · · · · · · · · · · · · · ·

1. Having a clear vision of why you've chosen this path will make the hard spots easier to navigate.
2. Use your power and privilege to give back to your community, loved ones, and those in need.
3. Make a conscious choice about what you want graduate school to be about. Make meaning of the setbacks in a way that motivates you forward.

Examining Regrets

Psychology graduate school is not right for everybody, and even the most motivated and excited graduate student will have doubts. Along the way, you'll surely have second thoughts, misgivings, or regrets. For most of you, those will be a function of passing stresses or disappointments. But for others, you might be right that this is not the field for you or that you're not in the right program.

> I constantly have second thoughts about choosing a PhD rather than pursuing a master's or PsyD program. The PhD route is so stressful and draining that I often wonder if I'm making the right choice.
>
> —Second-year public PhD student

> I don't have regrets about choosing to pursue graduate school in psychology. Although at times I worry about the time, energy, and money that have gone into my education.
>
> —Third-year private PsyD student

> The only regret I have is that I decided from a young age that I would pursue a career in psychology (age 14). I may not have had as much time to explore other career options, but I am very happy with my choice and continue to enjoy what I am learning, who I work with, and the type of work involved with graduate school in psychology.
>
> —Third-year public PhD student

Once or twice a year, I meet with a doctoral student who is questioning whether they should quit the program and do something different or apply to a different program. Sometimes these thoughts are related to program fit, finances, relationship issues, or misgivings about the field. Usually these are short-term feelings that arise during stressful times, but sometimes they aren't. Any decision to change one's path should be considered seriously and with a great deal of reflection before jumping ship. A personal therapist is great for that, as are supportive and helpful faculty members who will shoot straight with you. In the end, you're the only one who knows what's right for you, so grappling with a decision to leave can be a very painful and lonely time. No matter what, I urge you to slow down on making any decision without some time and distance. Often a student can take a leave of absence and return with some degree of clarity or perspective (or they can see clearly that returning is not for them). As a variant on the old adage, "Don't just do something—sit there."

I wouldn't say I have regrets about choosing my current path, but given the option to go back in time and choose the same route or a different one, I'm not sure what decision I would make. I would probably choose to do it the same, but I think it would take me a while to settle on that choice. The road has been a lot bumpier than I expected, but I would probably choose familiar discomfort over the unknown. Every program will be challenging. Life happens. I don't think it would be better if I had made a different choice. Maybe it was better not knowing how hard it would be.

—Lindsey, predoctoral intern, public PhD student

I sometimes have doubts. It feels like the reward is not worth the struggle, pain, and identity attacks from the academy.

—Third-year public PhD student

There have been times I have doubted myself and questioned whether or not this was the right path, but I do not have any regrets about pursuing my degree. However, I do have regrets about the steps along the way. If I could go back in time, I would not have chosen to pursue a concurrent, additional master's degree or other outside certifications. I would not have volunteered to do so many tasks outside of what was required of me. I would have held better boundaries with my family in terms of their needs from me. However, I am here now and doing my best to complete my PhD, because I know it is what I am meant to do.

—Summer, sixth-year public PhD student

With Great Power Comes Great Responsibility

If you're a graduate student in psychology, you're a member of a privileged bunch. Admissions can be brutally competitive, it's often very expensive, and you've needed to be excessively brilliant to get where you are. It's likely that your wacko family has been supportive of your education (even if they don't understand it) and that you have had the time and resources to reach for graduate school. Having an advanced degree puts you in rarified company, with only a small fraction of the population ever making it to where you are. A graduate degree gives you a whole bunch of freedom and oodles of power to shape your life and that of others.

What you do with that power is up to you. For some, just having a career that's personally rewarding and financially stable is enough. You can get a good job that will afford you more security than most people have. In and of itself, that's a great goal because for those of you who have experienced instability in your lives, you know that stability can't be overrated.

With my degree, I hope to have meaningful work. I hope to be able to provide for myself and those close to me while doing work that I am proud of. I hope to be able to contribute to and witness healing. It's such an honor when people let you into their lives and I hope to serve them and expand my own worldview.

—Natalie, third-year private PsyD student

I hope to become a licensed psychologist and work with underserved populations, primarily women and children. I would also like to work with emerging adults, who are at a crossroads in their lives, navigating individuation and integration into their new adult lives.

—Summer, sixth-year public PhD student

For others, their degree and the power that comes with it offer an opportunity to shake things up a little bit. As a younger generation of psychologists, the future of the discipline lies in your hands, and you can shape the field in ways that make sense to you. Power and privilege can be used to give voice to those who lack access to services, education, and safety. Power and privilege can be used to identify inequality and oppression. Power and privilege can change how psychology is practiced, delivered, and considered by society. My hope is that you'll continue to push forward with those visions because we need your perspective to grow and continue to be responsive to the needs of others.

The main thing that I hope my degree will allow me to do is to help shift academia into the radical place that I envision it can be. I want it to be a place that is representative of marginalized communities and that it is used to tell the stories of these communities and to help improve their conditions. I hope that I can make therapy into something that is for the people and not just rich, White people, but others who need mental health care.

—Second-year public PhD student

I hope to enter academia and continue to work on researching supports to help marginalized and underserved populations in the U.S. I hope that my degree will make a difference in the lives of others because I want to work closely with underrepresented undergraduate and graduate students and help more underrepresented students enter the field.

—Third-year public PhD student

I know that having a PhD is a privilege, and for me that means I need to be intentional about what I do with it. I would like to use my position to advocate for underrepresented populations and to draw attention to those topics and issues that are sometimes easier to ignore than to sit with. As a psychologist I am in a position to shine a light on some of those dark places, whether it be with clients in therapy, in a classroom with students, or with colleagues.

—Fourth-year public PhD student

In the spirit of making the most of your responsibility, I urge you to find a way to give back. No matter what your journey has been like, there have been others in your life who have gotten you to where you are. Inspirational teachers, loving parents, and caring mentors may have offered you support and confidence to pursue things that might have felt out of reach. If possible, it's a wonderful gesture to reach out and thank them (when I got tenure, I sent an email to my eighth-grade science teacher to thank her for her inspiration; she was sweet enough to pretend that she remembered me). Reach out with gratitude and be clear about what you have done with the gifts that others have given to you.

The other way of giving back is to pay it forward. Be the inspirational teacher or supportive family member for others who are at a different part of their journey. Many of you will teach undergraduate students during grad school, and you can give a real gift to the field by singling out bright students and giving them a push forward. You can also look for opportunities to connect with students at your undergrad alma mater and answer questions they might have about applying to graduate school or suggest books that they might read about what graduate school is really like.[2] Finally, there might be panels of graduate students for undergrads to help them understand how to apply to graduate school. If your department doesn't have one, put one together!

Recognizing that you have power and privilege also means that it's important to give to those who lack a voice. Too much of our culture neglects marginalized populations, but, as psychologists, we have a particular responsibility to offer what we can to those who have little. If you're headed toward a clinical career, make sure that you have a number of low-fee or free clients, waive a few copays, and consult widely in your community for free. If you're an academic, support students who have faced particular challenges due to diversity factors or other challenges. Giving aid to those who have faced greater marginalization, stigma, or barriers to success helps all of us and will do a great service with the degree you have earned.

I am particularly passionate about LGBTQ topics and hope to continue to educate on, and advocate for, gender minority rights and inclusion. I hope to use my degree in clinical and didactic capacities to spread compassion and understanding among providers and the public, as well as instill hope and empowerment in those who are marginalized and invalidated by so many.

—Natasha, fourth-year private PsyD student

---

[2] I can think of one offhand that's pretty decent.

One, Five, and Eight Years

Part of finding your lighthouse is remembering your visions for the future. As you work hard in graduate school, your life can often get reduced to the next paper, next client, next milestone, and so forth. In the spirit of pulling back, let's consider the future. In Chapter 9, I urged you to imagine your future as a way of contextualizing your professional development. Do you see yourself working for someone else, engaged in research, having a family, living abroad, or selling bagels? Once we have a big vision for the future, we can start to get a little more specific.

In the next five years, I hope to be really close to finishing my degree. I hope to have started a family, and I hope to feel more grounded in who I am.

—Second-year public PhD student

I'll be graduating soon. I've put off a lot of important personal milestones to be in graduate school. In the next five years, my hope is to establish a small private practice that will allow me the flexibility to start a family and start saving for a house. I'd like to be living with that mythical work/life balance I hear so many people talking about.

—Lauren, predoctoral intern, public PhD student

When I work with our first-year grad school class, I have them list personal, professional, and social goals for increments of one, five, and eight years. I call this exercise One, Five, Eight (super clever, right?). Personal goals might include learning to play guitar, running a marathon, learning to cook, going to clown college, and so on. Examples of professional goals include getting an internship, gaining experience with eating disorders, publishing a paper, or landing an academic job. Finally, social goals include things like dating, spending time with grandparents, making friends, getting married, and so forth. I have students list it all out in a table like this:

TABLE 12.1

	Personal	Professional	Social
One year from now			
Five years from now			
Eight years from now			

In eight years, I would like to have started my family, have a position as a staff psychologist at a college counseling center, and be spending my free time outdoors. I hope by then I will have the work/life balance that has not always been possible during graduate school.

—Fourth-year public PhD student

In five years, I would like to finish my PhD, earn my license, establish a private practice, and possibly teach.

—Summer, sixth-year public PhD student

I urge you to take some time and fill in a one-, five-, and eight-year plan table. Of course it'll change drastically over time, but it'll be more clarifying than you think it will be. Even more, fill a table out each year and see what changes and what doesn't. The things that don't change are good lighthouse material and should be signals about what's really important to you.

In the next eight years, I hope to have a family, including children. I hope to be at the beginning stages of my career as a professor and psychologist. I hope to have built a home somewhere.

—Second-year public PhD student

The Meaning of Graduate Studenting

There are as many reasons for going to graduate school as there are graduate students. Each of you has your own motivations, histories, and passions. And each one of you gets to decide what graduate school will *mean* to you. You can't change the milestones, you can't change the stresses, you can't change the requirements, but you can decide what attitude you bring and what meaning you make of it. For some, it's merely another few years of education to get to a desired outcome. For others, it's meaningful in and of itself to pursue knowledge and learn things of interest. In *Man's Search for Meaning*, Viktor Frankl (1946/2006) reminds us that difficulties are inevitable and that we can only shape how we approach those difficulties and make sense of them. Graduate school is no different. Remembering that you are building a life, building a career, positioning yourself to give back, shaping the future of the field, or merely working to provide for your future family will lend meaning to those parts of the journey that feel so tedious.

To me, being a graduate student means that the majority of your focus is on pursuing your degree, and you have to have a tunnel vision to get there.

—Second-year public PhD student

Being a graduate student is a learning and growing position. I LOVE the challenge that comes with developing skills and knowledge, but it is also totally scary. Being a graduate student for me can be boiled down to managing doubts, insecurities, and the drive to take advantage of every growth opportunity available. I get so excited about learning new things, I have had to reel myself in so I do not get overwhelmed with too many responsibilities. Then there are things that I have felt pushed into learning that bring up so much doubt that I have to remind myself I can do it. It is both of those things.

—Fourth-year public PhD student

Consider what you'd like your graduate school journey to be like. Do you want to see yourself as an instrument of change in the world? Do you want to see yourself as a bookish thinker who is doggedly pursuing knowledge? Do you want to see yourself as a downtrodden student who is slaving away under an authoritarian faculty? Do you want to see yourself as investing in a future vision of yourself and your life? Do you want to see yourself as a member of a community who will serve as a role model to members of disenfranchised groups? There are many more ways of making meaning of this part of your journey; some of them will make the journey longer, and some will make it shorter. Find a way to make meaning of this time and be open to changes in how you think about what it means.

Being a graduate student means you're miserable a lot of the time and you feel financially strapped and often uncared for by your university and undervalued by society as a whole, but it also means you have the opportunity to pursue your career goals and dedicate yourself fully to your passion.

—Third-year public PhD student

Being a graduate student means many things to me, but one of the best things about it is that you have a socially acceptable identity for five or more years as you explore what is most meaningful to you. The setup provides ample opportunity for personal development.

—Peter, fourth-year private PsyD student

Being a graduate student means trading right now for later. It means prioritizing the future. It's almost like a construction project. You spend years building a house for your future self. It takes a long time and a lot of hard work. Once you start, you've got to find a way to finish it. There may be times when it looks like a hot mess to passersby. There will be setbacks. You'll find ways to deal with unexpected hurdles because you have to. There isn't another choice. You can't move into a half-finished house. You keep going until you finish what you started, and then you move in and start building a life. It becomes a vessel for everything else.

—Lindsey, predoctoral intern, public PhD student

Being a graduate student means devoting oneself to not only a field of study, but to embodying and becoming an expert in that field of study. It is a complete immersion in a process of learning and experiencing a particular area of study and practice. It also means learning to balance that immersion with one's personal life and maintaining one's sense of self through that process. Being a graduate student is not for everyone; it takes dedication, persistence, humility, engagement, and acceptance of failure while still maintaining hope for success.

—Summer, sixth-year public PhD student

The Future of Psychology

Part of finding meaning is not only having a vision for yourself but also having a vision for our field. Your professors (myself included) might not always be the best judges of what the future of the field will be like. We're a little entrenched and invested in how things are. I think we can all share a vision of greater reach, reducing disparity, and helping those who are suffering. I'm just not sure we all have the same vision for how to get there. Part of your journey as a grad student is having some vision for how you'd like the field to be and what role you'd like to play in that vision.

If I have it my way, psychology will be accessible to all and prioritized as much as physical health. Psychology will be reflective of the population it serves.

—Second-year public PhD student

Our world is at a complex place in history with aggressively competing ideologies and very little constructive dialogue. Advances in technology have brought about some degree of increased fragmenting and isolation in addition to the marvelous gifts of communication and sharing of information. What is psychology's role in the complexity of the modern climate, and more directly, what is *your* role? Can you have a vision for yourself as a psychologist that moves us all forward? What is your role in making the world a better place for everyone?

In the United States specifically, given where we are at socially and politically, psychology and its role in society is evolving at a rapid pace. My hope is that the field of psychology adapts to our needs, grows in its openness and accessibility, and stands up to bureaucracy, oppression, and bigotry.

—Summer, sixth-year public PhD student

Hopefully psychology will be more accessible. I still see the field as catering predominantly to a very small subset of the population. I also hope the gap between research and practice can be reduced. Both are necessary for the field to have a positive impact.

—Fourth-year public PhD student

I believe positive psychology will one day be so embedded in psychology that it will not be considered its own branch. I would hope that therapy would become normalized in this country to the extent that stigma is reduced and people do not feel afraid or embarrassed to say they are seeing a therapist. I also hope that the field will be much more diverse in terms of clinicians and researchers than it is now, and that research will be readily available that isn't based on a predominantly White middle-class population/ideas/values.

—Third-year public PhD student

· · · · · · · · · · · · · · · · · · **Tips and Strategies** · · · · · · · · · · · · · · · · · ·

1. On a yearly basis, complete a one-year, five-year, and eight-year plan for professional, personal, and social goals.
2. Reach out to those who have helped you get to where you are and thank them.
3. Find ways to pay it forward. Be the inspiration to someone who can follow in your footsteps.

· ·

Graduate school is a long and challenging journey, but it is (or can be) a wonderful and fulfilling time in your life. There are good and honest reasons that you have chosen this path, this career, and this life. Keeping track of those reasons is a vital part of what you need to succeed in graduate school. There will be times of loneliness, setback, frustration, and exhaustion, but remembering your lighthouse and your sense of meaning will keep you headed in the right direction. Stay connected to who you are, where you're from, and what's gotten you to this point, and the rest will fall in line. Be honored to be a part of a long tradition of scholarship, and follow your passions to do good things in the world.

It is an exciting time to be in the field, and I am honored to represent it.

—Natasha, fourth-year private PsyD student

References

Frankl, V. E. (2006). *Man's search for meaning.* Boston, MA: Beacon Press. (Original work published 1946)

Hayes, S. C., Strosahl, K. D., & Wilson, K. G. (2011). *Acceptance and commitment therapy: Practice of mindful change* (2nd ed.). New York, NY: Guilford.

Index

About the Author

Steven R. Smith, PhD, is a licensed clinical psychologist and faculty member in the Department of Counseling, Clinical, and School Psychology and the College of Creative Studies at the University of California, Santa Barbara. He teaches, supervises, and serves as director of clinical training for the APA-accredited combined doctoral program. He also maintains a small private practice. His research and clinical interests include psychological assessment, the psychological needs of athletes, and psychotherapy for men and boys. He is married and the father of two and is an avid trail runner.